GO KAMADO

GRILL · SMOKE · BAKE · ROAST
GO KAMADO

MORE THAN 100 RECIPES FOR YOUR CERAMIC GRILL

CHEF JJ BOSTON

ALPHA

CONTENTS

INTRODUCTION

While I was working as a personal chef, a client introduced me to his kamado grill and asked me to cook dinner that evening on it. The first time I used this grill, I fell in love with it. The ability to control the temperature and the moisture in the heat are two things you don't see in traditional grills and ovens. I quickly adopted the kamado-style grill as my sole choice for presenting personal dinners and backyard experiences.

I love this style of grill because of its versatility, durability, and predictability. I've used the kamado to stretch the boundaries for hundreds of recipes in many variations. I've fed thousands of clients with my recipes and now I've collected my favorite ones into a single book for you to enjoy.

The recipes in this book highlight the diverse abilities of the kamado grill and give you a new perspective on the ingredients used. You can grill, bake, roast, and smoke foods, creating meals with deliciously unique tastes. With these different types of heat and cooking techniques—all detailed in separate sections in this book—you can cook virtually anything you want. And this book will show you how!

Chef JJ Boston

KAMADO ESSENTIALS

WHAT IS A KAMADO GRILL?

Your kamado grill is more than just something to use for a backyard barbecue. Known for its distinct egg-shaped silhouette and thick ceramic walls, this versatile charcoal-fueled cooker is an efficient way to grill, smoke, roast, and bake almost anything.

Ancient origins

The modern kamado grill has roots in Japan, where clay-oven cooking has been practiced for centuries. The word kamado (literally "place for the cauldron") can be used to refer to stoves or cooking ranges. In ancient Japan, clay cooking ranges called "kamado" were fueled by wood or charcoal and had dampers to control airflow. Modern kamado grills most closely resemble a style of clay, charcoal-fueled rice cooker with a removable dome-shaped lid called a "mushikamado."

Kamado-style grills were introduced to the United States after World War II, when American servicemen brought the concept back from Japan. By the 1960s, early versions of the kamado grill were commercially available in the United States. Like their contemporary counterparts, these early models offered a great deal of versatility in cooking, but they were made of porcelain and considerably more fragile than the kamado grills manufactured today. The high heat caused them to crack easily, and they were cumbersome to move.

> " The kamado is an all-in-one backyard barbecue grill that's easy to use and delivers consistent, delicious results. "

Kamado today

In recent years, the modern kamado grill has gained popularity and transitioned from a high-end niche product to one that's available at most hardware and home improvement stores. Sometimes called "ceramic grills" or "ceramic cookers," modern kamado grills are usually made from insulated ceramic. Unlike the clay used in earlier designs, the ceramic used in modern grills is extremely durable and designed to resist cracking. Although they might vary in color and size, all kamado grills share the same basic structure and functionality. More expensive models are typically made with higher-quality materials and might come with a lifetime guarantee.

The only grill you need

A kamado combines the utility of a charcoal kettle grill with the performance of a dedicated smoker, making it ideal for any backyard cooking. The thick walls of the kamado grill hold in heat, allowing the grill to maintain temperature for hours at a time. This capability makes it perfect for low, slow smoking and braising. The egg-shaped design of the kamado facilitates airflow and efficient use of fuel, allowing it to reach and maintain high temperatures. The upper and lower vents allow for precise control of airflow, which regulates the temperature.

HOW THE KAMADO GRILL WORKS

With its thick ceramic walls and egg-shaped design, the kamado can do far more than a traditional kettle grill or gas grill. Cook directly over the flame or cook indirectly by deflecting the heat and creating an oven-like space with even heat distribution.

Parts of the grill

There are many different kamado grills on the market—from modest tabletop models to enormous oval-shaped versions. Regardless of size or shape, all kamado grills share the same basic parts and functionality.

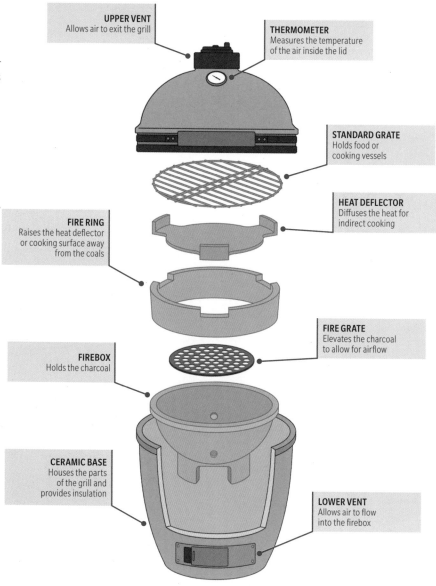

UPPER VENT
Allows air to exit the grill

THERMOMETER
Measures the temperature of the air inside the lid

STANDARD GRATE
Holds food or cooking vessels

HEAT DEFLECTOR
Diffuses the heat for indirect cooking

FIRE RING
Raises the heat deflector or cooking surface away from the coals

FIRE GRATE
Elevates the charcoal to allow for airflow

FIREBOX
Holds the charcoal

CERAMIC BASE
Houses the parts of the grill and provides insulation

LOWER VENT
Allows air to flow into the firebox

Two types of heat

There are two ways to configure your grill: direct heat and indirect heat. The type of heat you use depends on what you're making, how much time you have, and what flavors you want in your finished dish. Every recipe in this book clearly states which type of heat to use and when you need to convert from one to the other.

Some larger grills can be configured for direct and indirect heat at once, but most models can only effectively use one type of heat setup at a time.

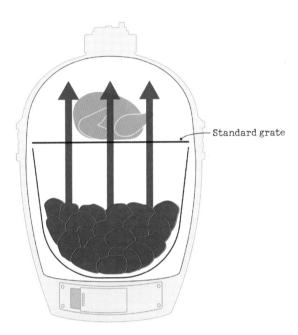

Standard grate

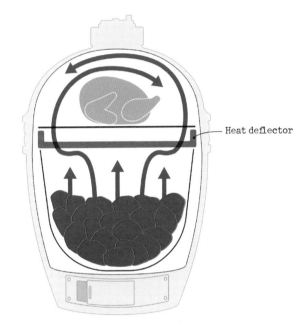

Heat deflector

Direct heat

This is the setup most people envision when they think about cooking on a grill. In the direct heat setup, food is placed on a grate directly above the burning coals and heat contacts the food from below. Direct heat is often used at higher temperatures and is the best way to sear meat and achieve quintessential grill marks, but it can cause uneven cooking.

Use direct heat for:

- Grilling
- Searing

Indirect heat

The indirect heat setup is what gives the kamado its versatility. In this configuration, a heat deflector is placed over the burning coals, diffusing the heat evenly within the grill. Cooking with indirect heat is similar to cooking in an oven. The heat surrounds the food rather than being concentrated on one spot. The ceramic walls absorb and retain heat.

Use indirect heat for:

- Smoking
- Roasting
- Baking

COOKING SURFACES & VESSELS

All kamado grills come with a standard stainless steel grate, which you can use for a wide range of applications, but there are other surfaces and vessels that can enhance the capabilities of your grill and give you more flexibility when cooking.

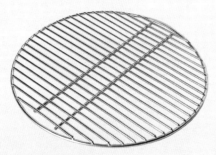

Standard grate

This stainless steel grate comes with your grill and can serve many different functions when cooking. For example, you can cook food directly on the grate, and you can also use the grate to hold a Dutch oven or skillet above the coals. Stainless steel doesn't get as hot as cast iron and won't hold heat as well.

Multi-tiered grate

Grates with multiple levels are designed to increase the surface area of your grill, giving you more space for large quantities of food. The multi-tiered grate is typically used for indirect cooking, such as roasting or smoking. There are many styles of multi-tiered grates available. Choose one that appeals to you.

Cast iron grate

Cast iron heats slowly but retains heat well, making it ideal for achieving perfect grill marks. In most cases, you'll want to install the cast iron grate before you preheat the grill.

Cast iron griddle

A two-sided cast iron griddle provides two cooking surfaces in one. The ridged side allows drippings to drain away, while the flat side allows food to cook in its juices. Install the griddle before the grill preheats.

V-rack

Racks are used when smoking or roasting to elevate the cooking meat and allow juices to run off into a drip pan. The V-shaped design is able to hold large pieces of meat in place, especially poultry.

Pizza stone

Ceramic pizza stones are preheated on the grill, absorbing the heat and creating a hot surface for baking pizzas and other types of bread as well as ensuring a crisp, well-browned bottom.

Dutch oven

The Dutch oven is an ideal vessel for braising and for making soups and stews. Purchase an uncoated cast iron Dutch oven—the type used for campfires. Dutch ovens intended for kitchen use, such as those with ceramic coatings, might not be able to withstand the high temperatures of the kamado grill.

Skillet

A cast iron skillet is an extremely versatile piece of cookware that can be used for sauces, stir-fries, baking—and much more. Like all cast iron cookware, it heats slowly but retains heat well. Place the cast iron skillet on a standard grate or a cast iron grate and allow it to preheat with the grill.

Other helpful cooking vessels

Drip pan
This pan is set under a grate or rack to catch the drippings from cooking meat. A simple disposable aluminum baking pan works well, although many manufacturers sell drip pans specifically designed for their grills.

Baking dishes
There are many types of baking dishes available to use in the kamado—often made from cast iron. You can also use inexpensive disposable aluminum baking pans for many baked dishes. Avoid using glass or ceramic dishes intended for kitchen ovens.

STARTING THE GRILL

Building a strong fire is key to grilling success with your kamado. The goal is to create a core of heat deep in the grill that will burn steadily and efficiently. For the best performance, use all-natural hardwood lump charcoal—not charcoal briquettes.

What do you need?

- **Natural hardwood lump charcoal**
- **Natural charcoal starter**
- **Ash rake**
- **Lighter**
- **Gloves**

TIP
Load the charcoal the same way every time—regardless of what cooking technique you plan to use. That's how you get consistent results.

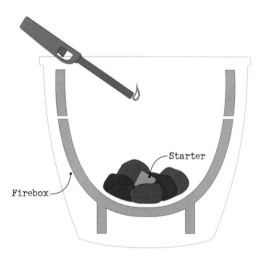

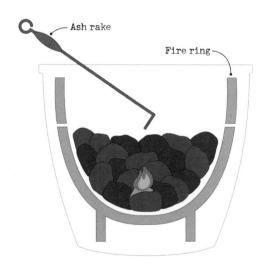

1 Light the starter. To create a core of heat, start the fire from the lowest point possible. Add a few chunks of charcoal to the bottom of the firebox. Nestle the charcoal starter among the coals. Light the charcoal starter using a wand-style lighter.

2 Add charcoal. Once the starter is burning steadily, add more charcoal, taking care not to pack it in tightly or smother the starter. Add charcoal until it reaches the rim of the ceramic fire ring, using the ash rake to move the charcoal around so it's evenly distributed.

Vents are fully open

Smoke dissipates when grill is hot

3 **Close the grill.** Once several coals are burning, close the grill lid, leaving the top and bottom vents fully open. If you're using indirect heat, first install the heat deflector and then install any cooking surfaces that need to preheat before you close the lid. This allows those elements to also get up to temperature.

4 **Watch and wait.** At first, visible white smoke will come from the top of the grill. This smoke will begin to disappear as the grill heats. Monitor the thermometer for at least 20 minutes. Once the grill reaches the needed temperature, partially close the vents to maintain that temperature.

Not getting hot?

If you're having trouble keeping the fire going or if your grill isn't reaching the needed temperature, try these troubleshooting tips.

Give the fire more air. If the charcoal is packed too tightly or the vents aren't fully open, your fire won't get the air it needs. Check that the vents are open and free of ash buildup and that the charcoal pieces aren't too small. (Large chunks will allow for more airflow.)

Give the fire more fuel. If you have plenty of airflow and still aren't creating enough heat, you might not have enough fuel. Be sure the charcoal reaches the rim of the ceramic fire ring.

Calibrate the thermometer. Improper calibration of the thermometer will result in an inaccurate temperature reading. Test your thermometer by placing the stem in boiling water. It should read 212°F (100°C) when calibrated.

CONTROLLING THE TEMPERATURE

A high-quality kamado grill can achieve and maintain temperatures ranging from 225°F (107°C) to 750°F (400°C). Heat is controlled by airflow through both vents. More airflow will increase the heat; less airflow will lower the heat.

Airflow controls the temperature

A fire needs fuel and oxygen to burn. Once the fire is lit, controlling the airflow is how you control the heat. Air enters the bottom vent and exits through the top vent. Opening the vents means more air and thus more heat; closing them means less air and heat.

Close to cool, open to heat

Once the grill reaches temperature, close both vents halfway. This will restrict the airflow, allowing enough oxygen to maintain the temperature but not so much that the heat increases. If the grill has gotten too hot, close both vents a little bit more. If the grill isn't hot enough, open both vents a little more. Adjust the vents in tandem, and give the fire time to react.

Don't assume the temperature shown on the gauge is always accurate. Because the gauge measures the air temperature within the lid, it can be affected by opening and closing the grill lid.

> " Make adjustments within 20 to 30 minutes of lighting the grill. Once a fire is well established, it takes time to reduce the temperature. "

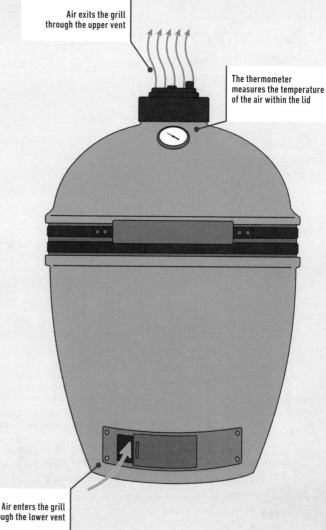

Air exits the grill through the upper vent

The thermometer measures the temperature of the air within the lid

Air enters the grill through the lower vent

Finding the right position

Setting the temperature of a grill isn't like turning a knob on your oven. There isn't a dial with temperature settings you can select. Instead, it will take a bit of practice and finesse to learn how to reach and maintain the correct temperature. In most circumstances, adjusting the vents in tandem will allow you to get within 5 to 10 degrees of the needed temperature.

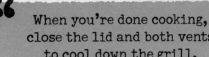

> When you're done cooking, close the lid and both vents to cool down the grill. It might take many hours for a hot grill to cool completely.

Mostly closed
Closing both vents most of the way will restrict airflow and lower the temperature. Vents might be kept mostly closed in order to maintain temperatures below 300°F (149°C), such as for smoking.

Partially open
Once your grill reaches temperature, adjust the vents so they're partially open. This position is where your vents should be to maintain temperatures between 300°F (149°C) and 500°F (260°C).

Fully open
Open the vents fully when lighting the grill and when cooking with maximum heat, such as for thin-crust pizza. As long as the vents remain open, the temperature will continue to rise to about 750°F (400°C).

 # SAFETY FIRST

Cook closed and burp to open
Unlike a charcoal kettle grill, the kamado grill is designed to stay closed while cooking. Opening the lid frequently interferes with the grill's ability to maintain a consistent temperature. When you need to open the lid, "burp" it by opening it just few inches for about 5 seconds before opening the lid fully. This allows oxygen to enter the grill slowly and prevents backdraft.

Beware of the backdraft
When the grill is hot, opening the lid quickly can cause backdraft (also called flashback). This is a dangerous surge of explosive heat created by introducing air to an oxygen-starved fire. The risk of backdraft is greatest when the grill is hot and the vents are restricting airflow, but you should make a habit of burping the grill whenever you open it.

TECHNIQUES:
GRILLING

Grilling on your kamado is simple and easy. Its ceramic design absorbs energy and creates an optimal environment for grilling and searing. Grilling is done at temperatures between 400°F (204°C) and 600°F (315°C) using direct heat. A cast iron grate is ideal for grilling, but a standard grate will also work. Once the grill is hot and the grates are preheated, you're ready to grill any type of food. Helpful tools for grilling include tongs, hot gloves, and an instant-read thermometer.

1 Add a few chunks of charcoal to the bottom of the firebox. Nestle a charcoal starter among the coals. Light the charcoal starter using a wand-style lighter.

2 Once the starters are burning steadily, add more charcoal. Keep adding charcoal until they reach the rim of the ceramic fire ring.

3 Once several coals are burning, install a standard or cast iron grate. Close the lid of the grill, leaving the top and bottom vents fully open.

4 Once the grill reaches temperature, partially close the top and bottom vents to maintain that temperature. Place your food on the grate and close the lid. (Always keep the lid closed when cooking, even if the food only needs to cook for a few minutes.)

5 Turn the food as necessary using tongs or a metal spatula, and brush with sauce (if desired).

> **Keep the grill closed while grilling unless you're actively turning the food. Be sure to "burp" the lid when opening to prevent flashback.**

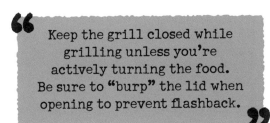

Standard grate

The stainless steel grate that comes standard with most kamado grills is a good grilling surface. However, because stainless steel doesn't retain heat as well as cast iron, it doesn't deliver pronounced grill marks.

Cast iron grate

Although it's heavy and takes time to heat, a cast iron grate is an ideal grilling surface because it holds in the heat, allowing the food to cook quickly and evenly and leaving behind distinct grill marks.

TECHNIQUES:
SMOKING

Smoking is where the kamado really shines. With its unique shape and ability to maintain consistent temperatures for long periods of time, the kamado keeps meat moist and tender while infusing it with a smoky flavor. Smoking is done at a low temperature, usually below 300°F (150°C), using indirect heat. Once the grill is hot, chunks of smoking wood are added to the hot coals. Smoking isn't just for meat and fish; you can add smoking wood to flavor any food—from nuts to vegetables. Helpful tools include tongs, hot gloves, and a remote leave-in thermometer.

> " Add just a few wood chunks at first, and adjust the amount as you learn what you like. Try combining different woods for more complex flavors. "

1 Add a few chunks of charcoal to the bottom of the firebox. Nestle a charcoal starter among the coals. Light the charcoal starter using a wand-style lighter, adding fresh charcoal if needed. Make sure the top and bottom vents are fully open and close the grill lid.

2 Once the thermometer reaches your target temperature between 225°F (107°C) and 300°F (150°C), open the lid and place a few chunks of smoking wood on the hot coals.

3 Install the heat deflector as well as a drip pan and standard grate (if using), and place your food on the grate. If using a rack and drip pan, place the meat on the rack, set the rack in the drip pan, and place this setup directly on the heat deflector.

4 Close the lid and close the top and bottom vents most of the way. Check the thermometer after 10 minutes to verify that it still reflects your desired temperature. If the grill is too hot, close the vents more. If the grill is too cool, open the vents slightly.

Standard grate and drip pan

A standard stainless steel grate is all you need for most smoking applications. Place a drip pan on the heat deflector below the grate to catch drippings.

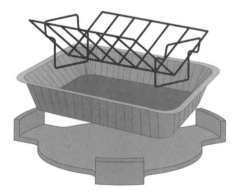

Rack and drip pan

A rack elevates the meat and ensures even smoking. Place the rack in a drip pan to catch drippings. You can also add stock, beer, or wine to the drip pan to further enhance the flavor of the smoked meat.

Using smoking wood

The kamado is fueled with charcoal, which means everything you cook will be touched with a smoke flavor. For a more pronounced smokiness, you can add chunks of smoking wood to the coals. Smoke is like any other seasoning; everyone has their own palate and preferences. Different types of wood vary in intensity—from lighter woods like cherry and apple, which can lend subtle fruity notes, to high-intensity mesquite, which infuses food with a robust smoky flavor. The type and amount of smoking wood you use will be dictated by personal preference.

Cherry wood

Grapevine wood

Hickory wood

	WOOD	DESCRIPTION	BEST FOR
LIGHT ↑	APPLE	Light and fruity, with a slightly sweet aroma. The lightest of all fruit woods.	pork, poultry
	CHERRY	Light smoke and sweet flavor; creates a smoke ring with a red hue.	pork, poultry, beef tenderloin
	ALDER	Light and subtle, slightly sweet. Similar to cedar in appearance and scent.	fish, light meats
	PEACH	Dense wood with a bittersweet aroma. The heaviest of all fruit woods.	pork, poultry, fish
	GRAPEVINE	Stronger than most fruit woods but with a similar sweetness.	beef, duck, wild game
	MAPLE	Medium smoke with a slight sweetness and mild bitterness.	fatty meats, seafood
	PECAN	Medium to strong smoke, with a slight nuttiness that pairs well with fruit woods.	wild game, pork, steak
	BOURBON BARREL	Medium smoke; made from white oak but sweeter and more fragrant.	red meat, wild game
	RED OAK	Strong but not overpowering, making it a great all-around smoking wood.	beef, lamb, sausage
	HICKORY	Strong, sweet flavor that works well for fattier meats but can be overpowering.	brisket, spare ribs, pork shoulder
↓ INTENSE	MESQUITE	Dense wood with a strong, bitter flavor and heavy smoke.	brisket, spare ribs, pork shoulder

TECHNIQUES:
ROASTING

Roasting is easy with your kamado. The unique shape and insulating properties of ceramic allow the grill to maintain accurate temperatures for long periods of time—even more accurate than the oven in your kitchen. Roasting is done at temperatures between 350°F (176°C) and 450°F (232°C) using indirect heat. Roasting is often done with large cuts of meat, but vegetables and fish are also delicious when roasted. Helpful tools for roasting include a multi-tiered grate, V-rack, drip pan, and remote leave-in thermometer.

> " A remote leave-in thermometer is essential for achieving perfectly cooked roasts. Look for models designed for use with grills. "

1 Add a few chunks of charcoal to the bottom of the firebox. Nestle a charcoal starter among the coals. Light the charcoal starter using a wand-style lighter.

2 Once the starters are burning steadily, add more charcoal. Keep adding charcoal until they reach the rim of the ceramic fire ring.

3 Once several coals are burning, install the heat deflector and a standard grate as well as any cookware that needs to preheat. Close the lid, leaving the top and bottom vents fully open.

4 When the grill reaches the needed temperature for roasting, partially close both vents to maintain that temperature. Place the meat on the grill—either in a rack with a drip pan or directly on the grate— and close the lid. Check the temperature after 10 minutes, and make adjustments if needed.

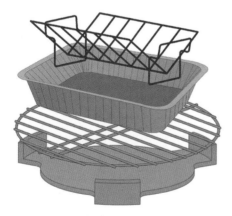

Standard grate, rack, and drip pan

Roasting large cuts of meat in a rack keeps them elevated, allowing the heat to surround the meat. A drip pan keeps the grill clean and catches drippings.

Standard grate and drip pan

Meat and vegetables can easily be roasted directly on a standard grate, with a drip pan below to catch juices. Add stock or wine to the drip pan for more flavor.

TECHNIQUES:
BAKING

Like roasting, baking is a cooking method that relies on surrounding food with dry, even heat at a consistent temperature. Anything that can be baked in a kitchen oven can be baked in a kamado—from breads and cakes to pies, casseroles, and pizza—as long as you use appropriate bakeware. Baking is done at temperatures between 300°F (149°C) and 425°F (218°C) using indirect heat. Pizzas typically bake at a higher temperature, above 500°F (260°C). Recommended bakeware includes a cast iron skillet or Dutch oven, a pizza stone, and disposable aluminum pans.

> " For best results, stick to all-metal bakeware, such as cast iron or aluminum pans. Ceramic, glass, and even stoneware can crack. "

1 Add a few chunks of charcoal to the bottom of the firebox. Nestle a charcoal starter among the coals. Light the charcoal starter using a wand-style lighter.

2 Once the starters are burning steadily, add more charcoal. Keep adding charcoal until they reach the rim of the ceramic fire ring.

3 Once several coals are burning, install a standard or cast iron grate. Close the lid, leaving the top and bottom vents fully open.

4 When the grill reaches the needed temperature for baking, partially close both vents to maintain that temperature. Place the food on the grate or pizza stone and close the lid. Check the temperature after 10 minutes, and make adjustments if needed.

Standard grate and skillet

A well-seasoned cast iron skillet can be used to bake breads, pies, cobblers, and casseroles. If your baked dish requires higher sides, a well-seasoned cast iron Dutch oven can also be used for baking.

Pizza stone

Ceramic pizza stones rest directly on the heat deflector and are preheated in the grill. They can be used for all kinds of breads, not just pizza. A pizza paddle is also useful for transferring pizza to and from the pizza stone.

WILD GAME

PREP TIME
3 HRS

COOK TIME
15–25 MINS

SERVES
8

HEAT
DIRECT
325°F (163°C)

COOKING SURFACE
CAST IRON GRATE
DUTCH OVEN

Succulent rabbit is brushed with rich hoisin sauce and grilled alongside a colorful succotash, infusing the medley of vegetables with flavor. Spicy pickled carrots complete the meal.

HOISIN GRILLED RABBIT
with succotash & pickled carrots

INGREDIENTS

2 rabbits, about 4lb (1.8kg)
  in total, quartered

¼ cup hoisin sauce

for the brine

⅔ cup kosher salt

⅔ cup packed light brown sugar

4 tbsp pickling spice

8 cups hot water

2 tbsp Chinese five-spice powder

for the pickled carrots

¼ cup sugar

½ cup rice vinegar

½ cup water

2 tbsp hot sauce

2lb (1kg) carrots, peeled

for the succotash

1 red bell pepper, left whole

2 ears of corn, shucked

2 tbsp extra virgin olive oil

1 cup diced red onion

1 large garlic clove, minced

1 cup fresh edamame, shelled

kosher salt and freshly ground
  black pepper

1 tbsp thinly sliced fresh basil

METHOD

1 To make the brine, in a large bowl, whisk together salt, brown sugar, pickling spice, and water until salt and sugar have dissolved. Add ice cubes a few at a time until the liquid is no longer hot. Stir in Chinese five-spice powder. Place rabbit pieces in a large resealable plastic bag and add brine to fully cover. (Any extra brine can be refrigerated and saved for a later use.) Refrigerate for 1 hour.

2 Preheat the grill to 325°F (163°C) using direct heat with a cast iron grate installed. Place carrots, pepper, and corn on the grate, close the lid, and grill until beginning to soften and char, about 6 to 8 minutes. Remove the vegetables from the grill, place a Dutch oven on the grate to heat, and close the lid. Once the vegetables are cool enough to handle, cut the kernels from the cobs, seed and dice pepper, and slice carrots into rounds.

3 To make the pickled carrots, in a small saucepan, combine sugar, vinegar, and water. Place on the stovetop over high heat and bring to a boil. Reduce heat to low and stir in the hot sauce. Remove from the heat. Pack the sliced carrots into several airtight containers and pour the hot pickling solution over the carrots to cover. Cover the containers with lids, let cool to room temperature, and refrigerate for at least 2 hours before using. (Pickled carrots can be made in advance and will keep for up to 6 months in the fridge.)

4 Remove rabbit from the brine and pat dry with paper towels. Lightly brush with hoisin sauce and place on the grate next to the Dutch oven. To the Dutch oven, add oil, onion, garlic, edamame, and grilled pepper and corn. Leave the Dutch oven uncovered, close the grill lid, and grill rabbit until the meat reaches an internal temperature of 160°F (71°C) and the onions are soft, about 10 to 15 minutes, turning the rabbit pieces once. Season the succotash with salt and pepper to taste and sprinkle with basil.

5 Remove rabbit and the Dutch oven from the grill and serve immediately with the pickled carrots.

PREP TIME
2 HRS

COOK TIME
10–15 MINS

SERVES
4

HEAT
DIRECT
400°F (204°C)

COOKING SURFACE
CAST IRON GRATE
CAST IRON SKILLET

Antelope is a lean red meat similar to venison but with a milder flavor. When marinated for tenderness and served with a rich, brandy-spiked sauce, these medallions will surely impress.

ANTELOPE MEDALLIONS
with brandy cream sauce

INGREDIENTS

2 antelope tenderloins, 2lb (1kg) in total, cut into 8 medallions

4 tbsp olive oil

for the marinade

3½ tsp extra virgin olive oil

½ tsp sesame oil

2 tbsp brandy

1 garlic clove, minced

⅛ tsp kosher salt

⅛ tsp ground black pepper

for the sauce

1 tbsp olive oil

1 shallot, minced

1 garlic clove, minced

¼ cup brandy

1 cup beef stock

2 tbsp heavy cream

1 tsp hot sauce

kosher salt and freshly ground black pepper

METHOD

1 To make the marinade, in a large bowl, whisk together olive oil, sesame oil, brandy, garlic, salt, and pepper. Place antelope in the marinade, cover with plastic wrap, and refrigerate for 2 hours.

2 Preheat the grill to 400°F (204°C) using direct heat with a cast iron grate installed and a cast iron skillet on the grate. Remove the medallions from the marinade, pat dry with paper towels, and coat with olive oil on all sides. Place the medallions on the grate (not in the skillet), close the lid, and grill until the internal temperature reaches 160°F (71°C), about 3 to 5 minutes per side, flipping once.

3 To make the sauce, in the hot skillet, heat oil until shimmering. Add shallot and garlic, and sauté until they begin to brown, about 2 minutes. Add brandy and flambé. (The heat of the pan should create a burst of flame.) When the flames subside, add stock, cream, and hot sauce. Close the lid and cook until the sauce has reduced to ¼ cup, about 5 to 8 minutes.

4 Remove the medallions from the grill, spoon sauce over top, and serve immediately.

TIP A reputable butcher will have access to wild game. If antelope is unavailable, you can use venison or even pork tenderloin in this recipe. Add peach, apricot, or oak wood chunks for a more smoky flavor.

PREP TIME **30 MINS**	COOK TIME **8-12 MINS**	SERVES **6**	HEAT **DIRECT** **425°F (218°C)**	COOKING SURFACE **CAST IRON GRATE**

Change your burger experience with lean, flavorful bison.
Mustard and hot sauce give these robust patties a spicy kick
that's tempered with sweet-and-tangy Thousand Island sauce.

BISON BURGERS
with Thousand Island sauce

INGREDIENTS

6 hamburger buns

2lb (1kg) ground bison

2 tbsp kosher salt

½ tbsp freshly ground coffee
 or instant coffee granules

2 tbsp Dijon mustard

4 tbsp Worcestershire sauce

2 tsp hot sauce, plus more
 as desired

for the sauce

6 tbsp ketchup

¼ cup mayonnaise

¼ cup finely chopped
 cornichon pickles

2 tsp white vinegar

½ tsp dry mustard

¼ tsp ground cayenne pepper

¼ tsp Old Bay seasoning

kosher salt and freshly ground
 black pepper

METHOD

1 To make the sauce, in a medium bowl, combine ketchup, mayonnaise, cornichons, vinegar, mustard, cayenne, and Old Bay seasoning. Taste and season well with salt and pepper, cover with plastic wrap, and refrigerate until ready to serve.

2 Preheat the grill to 425°F (218°C) using direct heat with a cast iron grate installed. Place hamburger buns face down on the grate and grill until they have grill marks, about 2 to 3 minutes. Remove from the grill and set aside.

3 In a large bowl, gently combine bison, salt, coffee grounds, mustard, Worcestershire sauce, and hot sauce. Form the mixture into 6 patties of equal size. Place the patties on the grate, close the lid, and grill until they reach desired doneness, about 4 to 6 minutes per side.

4 Remove the patties from the grill and place on the buns. Spoon the sauce over top and add desired toppings. Serve immediately.

TIP Soft, buttery brioche buns are a perfect choice for these boldly flavored burgers. For maximum flavor, lightly grill the buns and load up on toppings, such as lettuce, tomato, cheese, bacon, and avocado.

PREP TIME
7½ HRS

COOK TIME
42–60 MINS

SERVES
4

HEAT
**INDIRECT
500°F (260°C)**

COOKING SURFACE
CAST IRON GRATE

Tiny but full of flavor, these diminutive game birds are coated
with rice flour and roasted, yielding a delicately crisp skin.
A vinegar-based cabbage slaw complements the richness of the meat.

ROASTED QUAIL
with red wine sauce & tangy slaw

INGREDIENTS

8 quail, about 2lb (1kg) in total,
  left whole

4 cups rice flour

coarse kosher salt and freshly
  ground black pepper

for the slaw

½ cup rice wine vinegar

6 tbsp extra virgin olive oil

1½ tsp coarse kosher salt

1½ tsp freshly ground
  black pepper

1 head of green cabbage,
  shredded

2 tbsp chopped fresh flat-leaf
  parsley

for the brine

⅔ cup kosher salt

⅔ cup packed light brown sugar

4 tbsp pickling spice

8 cups hot water

for the sauce

1½ cups dry red wine

1 cup packed dark brown sugar,
  plus 2 tbsp

½ cup low-sodium soy sauce

4 tbsp finely grated fresh ginger

8 garlic cloves, minced

METHOD

1 To make the slaw, in a large bowl, whisk together vinegar, olive oil, salt,
and pepper. Add cabbage and parsley, then toss until well coated. Cover with
plastic wrap and refrigerate for at least 5 hours to allow the flavors to meld.

2 To make the brine, in a large bowl, whisk together salt, brown sugar, pickling
spice, and water until salt and sugar have dissolved. Add ice cubes a few at a time
until the liquid is no longer hot. Place quail in a large resealable plastic bag and
add brine to fully cover. (Any extra brine can be refrigerated and saved for a later
use.) Refrigerate for 1 hour.

3 Remove quail from the brine, pat dry with paper towels, and place on a baking
sheet. Coat liberally with rice flour, wrap tightly with plastic wrap, and refrigerate
for 1 hour.

4 To make the sauce, in a medium saucepan, combine wine, brown sugar, soy
sauce, ginger, and garlic. Place on the stovetop over medium-high heat and
bring to a boil. Reduce the heat to medium and simmer until the mixture has
thickened to the consistency of honey, about 35 to 40 minutes. Remove from
the heat and set aside.

5 Preheat the grill to 500°F (260°C) using indirect heat with a cast iron grate
installed. Place quail on the grate, close the lid, and roast without turning
until the internal temperature reaches 160°F (71°C), about 12 to 15 minutes.

6 Remove the birds from the grill, brush with the sauce, and sprinkle each quail with
salt and pepper. Serve warm with the remaining sauce and the slaw.

PREP TIME
30 MINS

COOK TIME
35–45 MINS

SERVES
4

HEAT
INDIRECT
425°F (218°C)

COOKING SURFACE
CAST IRON GRATE
CAST IRON SKILLET

Spice-rubbed alligator steaks are stuffed with a rich filling of savory sausage and sweet dates and then wrapped in bacon for more smoky flavor. A compound butter takes this dish to the next level.

STUFFED ALLIGATOR
with savory herbed butter

INGREDIENTS

4 alligator steaks, 6oz (170g) each
3 tbsp butter, melted
8 thin-cut bacon slices

for the stuffing
8oz (225g) pork sausage, such as Italian sausage or ground pork
½ cup dates, pitted and chopped
¼ cup water
1½ cups sugar

for the butter
4oz (110g) salted butter
⅛ tbsp minced shallot
¼ tbsp minced fresh flat-leaf parsley
⅛ tbsp brown gravy mix
1¼ tbsp lemon juice
1 tsp Worcestershire sauce
¼ tsp Tabasco sauce

for the rub
1 tsp kosher salt
1 tbsp paprika
1 tsp ground cayenne pepper
½ tsp ground black pepper
½ tsp ground white pepper
½ tsp dried thyme
½ tsp dried oregano
½ tsp dried chives
1 tsp garlic powder

METHOD

1 Preheat the grill to 425°F (218°C) using indirect heat with a cast iron grate installed and a cast iron skillet on the grate.

2 To make the stuffing, place sausage in the hot skillet, close the lid, and cook until browned, about 10 minutes. Transfer sausage to a large bowl and set aside, reserving the drippings in the skillet. Add dates, water, and sugar to the skillet, and cook until the mixture begins to thicken, about 15 minutes. Remove the skillet from the grill and fold in the browned sausage.

3 To make the butter, in a small bowl, combine all the butter ingredients. Roll the mixture into a log, wrap tightly with plastic wrap, and freeze for 20 minutes.

4 To make the rub, in a small bowl, combine all the rub ingredients. Slice a small pocket into each steak and fill the cavity with some of the sausage stuffing. Brush each steak with melted butter, coat in the spice rub, and wrap with 2 bacon slices.

5 Place alligator on the grate, close the lid, and grill until the internal temperature reaches 160°F (71°C) and bacon has fully cooked, about 12 to 18 minutes, turning halfway through.

6 Remove alligator from the grill. Cut the butter into discs and place one on each steak. Serve immediately.

PREP TIME
45 MINS

COOK TIME
2½ HRS

SERVES
8

HEAT
**INDIRECT
250°F (121°C)**

COOKING SURFACE
**STANDARD GRATE
DUTCH OVEN**

For this hearty meat sauce, goat is braised in beer, cola, and aromatics before being shredded and simmered with wine and tomatoes. Serve it over rigatoni for comfort food at its best.

SMOKED GOAT BOLOGNESE

INGREDIENTS

1½lb (680g) boneless goat leg

kosher salt and freshly ground black pepper

1–2 tsp sweet smoked paprika

1 medium yellow onion, chopped

4 garlic cloves, chopped

3 celery stalks, diced

2 carrots, diced

1½ cups beer

1½ cups cola

1lb (450g) dried rigatoni

olive oil

for the sauce

1 tbsp olive oil

1 white onion, diced

4 garlic cloves, minced

15oz (425g) can crushed tomatoes

1 cup red wine

1 tsp fresh oregano, minced

½ cup heavy cream

to smoke

cherry or wine barrel wood chunks

METHOD

1 About 2 to 3 hours before cooking, coat goat leg liberally with salt, pepper, and a light (but thorough) dusting of paprika. Cover with plastic wrap and allow to come to room temperature.

2 Preheat the grill to 250°F (121°C). Once hot, add the wood chunks, then install the heat deflector and a standard grate with a Dutch oven on the grate. Add onion, garlic, celery, and carrots to the Dutch oven. Close the grill lid and sweat the vegetables for 5 minutes. Stir in beer and cola, and add goat leg.

3 Loosely cover the Dutch oven with aluminum foil, close the grill lid, and smoke until the internal temperature reaches 190°F (88°C), about 1 to 2 hours, checking the temperature every hour. Transfer goat leg to a large serving platter and let rest for 30 to 45 minutes, then shred the meat. Season with salt and pepper to taste. Set aside.

4 Cook the rigatoni on the stovetop according to package directions. Drain and rinse with cold water, and toss with a little olive oil to prevent sticking. Set aside.

5 To make the sauce, on the stovetop in a large skillet over medium heat, heat oil until shimmering. Add onions and garlic, and sauté until fragrant and beginning to brown, about 2 to 3 minutes. Add tomatoes, wine, and oregano. Cook until reduced by one-fourth, about 10 to 15 minutes.

6 Add shredded meat, cream, and cooked rigatoni to the skillet. Stir gently and cook until thick, about 5 to 7 minutes. Season with salt and pepper to taste, and serve warm.

BEEF

PREP TIME
30 MINS

COOK TIME
20-25 MINS

SERVES
4

HEAT
**DIRECT
425°F (218°C)**

COOKING SURFACE
**STANDARD GRATE
CAST IRON SKILLET**

These irresistible Asian-inspired tacos are stuffed with savory strips of beef, grilled and shredded cabbage, and tender mushrooms. The filling is tossed with hoisin sauce and topped with cilantro.

ASIAN BEEF & MUSHROOM TACOS

INGREDIENTS

½ head of green cabbage

1lb (450g) flank or round steak, cut into very thin strips

kosher salt and freshly ground black pepper

3 tbsp vegetable oil, divided

1lb (450g) white mushrooms, sliced

4oz (110g) shredded carrots, fresh or pickled

⅓ cup hoisin sauce, plus more for serving

8 x 6-in (15.25-cm) flour tortillas

¼ cup chopped fresh cilantro

METHOD

1 Preheat the grill to 425°F (218°C) using direct heat with a standard grate installed and a cast iron skillet on the grate. Place cabbage on the grate (not in the skillet) cut side down, close the lid, and grill until beginning to soften and char, about 7 to 10 minutes. Remove cabbage from the grill and slice finely. Set aside.

2 Season beef well with salt and pepper. Add 2 tbsp oil to the hot skillet and heat until shimmering. Add beef and cook until the meat has browned on both sides, about 5 to 6 minutes, turning once. Transfer to a platter and set aside. Return the skillet to the grill.

3 Add the remaining 1 tbsp oil to the skillet and heat until shimmering. Add mushrooms and cook until they're tender and all the liquid has evaporated, about 5 minutes. Add carrots and sliced cabbage to the skillet and cook until beginning to soften, about 2 minutes, stirring once or twice. Add the hoisin sauce and beef, stir to coat, and cook for 1 minute more.

4 Remove the taco mixture from the grill. To serve, scoop an equal portion of the mixture into each tortilla and top with cilantro and more hoisin sauce (if desired).

PREP TIME
6–24 HRS

COOK TIME
6–12 MINS

SERVES
8

HEAT
**DIRECT
400°F (204°C)**

COOKING SURFACE
CAST IRON GRATE

The flavors of bold garlic and ginger are balanced by sweet pears in the spicy marinade that coats these ribs. Seek out flanken-style ribs, which are cut lengthwise across the rib bones.

KOREAN-STYLE BEEF SHORT RIBS

INGREDIENTS

3lb (1.4kg) flanken-style beef ribs, cut ¼-in (.5-cm) thick

for the marinade

1 medium ripe pear, peeled and diced

6 garlic cloves, roughly chopped

1 tbsp chili garlic sauce

1 tbsp minced fresh ginger

3 tbsp toasted sesame oil

6 tbsp sugar

2 tbsp rice vinegar

3 scallions, thinly sliced

kimchi (optional), to serve

METHOD

1 To make the marinade, in a food processor, combine pear, garlic, chili garlic sauce, ginger, sesame oil, sugar, and rice vinegar. Pulse until smooth, and stir in the scallions. Reserve ⅓ cup marinade.

2 Place ribs in a large resealable plastic bag and pour the remaining marinade over top. Squeeze out any excess air and refrigerate for 6 to 24 hours, turning once or twice.

3 Preheat the grill to 400°F (204°C) using direct heat with a cast iron grate installed. Place ribs on the grate, close the lid, and cook until browned, about 6 to 12 minutes, turning 2 to 3 times.

4 On the stovetop in a small saucepan over medium heat, warm the reserved marinade. Remove ribs from the grill, place on a large serving platter, and spoon the warmed marinade over top. Serve immediately with kimchi (if using).

Although you might be tempted to go with the shorter marinade time, if you refrigerate the ribs for 24 hours, this ensures the meat cooks properly and is tender—making for easier and better eating.

PREP TIME
30 MINS

COOK TIME
4¹⁄₂ HRS

SERVES
6

HEAT
DIRECT
375ºF (191ºC)

COOKING SURFACE
DUTCH OVEN

Searing this roast directly on the coals quickly locks in its juices, and a long simmer in a chipotle sauce infuses it with flavor. Serve piled on warm tortillas and topped with onion, cilantro, and lime.

BEEF BARBACOA
with chipotle sauce

INGREDIENTS

4lb (1.8kg) chuck-eye roast

2 bay leaves

kosher salt and freshly ground black pepper

6 x 6-in (15.25-cm) corn tortillas, warmed

for the sauce

2 tbsp vegetable oil

1 small white onion, finely sliced

6 garlic cloves, smashed

2 tsp ground cumin

½ tsp ground cloves

2 tsp dried oregano

4 chipotle peppers in adobo, roughly chopped, plus 2 tbsp adobo sauce

¼ cup apple cider vinegar

4 cups low-sodium chicken stock, divided

1 dried New Mexico pepper, seeds and stem removed

1 dried ancho pepper, seeds and stem removed

1 dried negro pepper, seeds and stem removed

2 tsp fish sauce

METHOD

1 Preheat the grill to 375°F (191°C) using direct heat with nothing but coals in the grill. Place roast directly on the coals and sear all sides until browned and the internal temperature reaches 160°F (71°C), about 3 to 5 minutes per side. Remove roast from the grill and set aside.

2 Install the heat deflector and place a Dutch oven on top. Close the top and bottom vents most of the way to lower the temperature to 325°F (163°C). To the hot Dutch oven, add oil, onion, and garlic, and cook until onions are well browned, about 10 minutes. Add cumin, cloves, and oregano, and cook until fragrant, about 30 seconds, stirring constantly. Add chipotle peppers, adobo sauce, vinegar, and 2 cups stock to the Dutch oven. Scrape up the browned bits from the bottom, and simmer until stock has reduced by about half, about 15 minutes. Transfer contents of the Dutch oven to a blender and return the Dutch oven to the grill.

3 Place dried peppers in a large saucepan and add remaining 2 cups chicken stock. Bring to a boil on the stovetop over high heat, reduce heat to low, and simmer until peppers are completely tender, about 15 minutes. Add the soaked peppers and their liquid to the blender with onion and chipotle mixture. Add the fish sauce. Purée until smooth, and set aside.

4 Place roast, bay leaves, and sauce in the Dutch oven. Cook until the internal temperature reaches 185°F (85°C), about 4 hours, turning occasionally. Discard bay leaves. Transfer roast to a serving platter and cover with aluminum foil. Return the Dutch oven to the grill and cook the remaining liquid until reduced to 1½ cups, about 5 minutes, stirring frequently.

5 Roast can be cut and served immediately, but for the best flavor, place roast and sauce in a sealable container and refrigerate for up to 5 days. When ready to serve, shred roast into chunks and transfer the meat and sauce to a large pot. On the stovetop over medium-high heat, bring to a simmer and cook, stirring gently, until beef is tender and coated in sauce, about 10 to 15 minutes.

PREP TIME
24 HRS

COOK TIME
15 HRS

SERVES
38

HEAT
INDIRECT
225°F (107°C)

COOKING SURFACE
STANDARD GRATE

A traditional Texas-style smoked brisket requires planning and preparation, but nothing compares to the tender, flavorful meat that results from hours of low-and-slow smoking.

SMOKED BEEF BRISKET

INGREDIENTS

1¼ cups sugar

⅔ cup ground black pepper

⅔ cup seasoned salt

⅔ cup kosher salt

2½ tbsp ground cayenne pepper

15lb (6.8kg) whole beef brisket, trimmed of fat

pickle slices (optional), to serve

BBQ sauce (optional), to serve

to smoke

post oak, hickory, or mesquite wood chunks

METHOD

1 In a medium bowl, combine sugar, pepper, seasoned salt, kosher salt, and cayenne. Rub brisket with the seasoning mixture. Wrap tightly with plastic wrap and refrigerate for 24 hours.

2 Preheat the grill to 225°F (107°C). Once hot, add the wood chunks, install the heat deflector, place a drip pan on top, and install a standard grate. Remove brisket from the fridge and allow to come to room temperature.

3 Place the brisket fat side up on the grate, close the lid, and smoke until the internal temperature reaches 160°F (71°C), about 5 to 7 hours. Remove brisket from the grill, wrap heavily in aluminum foil, and return to the grill to continue to cook until the internal temperature reaches 185°F (85°C), about 8 hours. (Check the texture of the meat for doneness throughout the cooking process). The total cook time is about 15 hours, or 1 hour per pound (approximately 2 hours per kilogram).

4 Transfer brisket to a serving platter and let rest for 20 minutes. Slice or shred the meat, and serve with pickle slices and BBQ sauce (if desired).

TIP Briskets can vary in size and shape, so pay attention to the thermometer, not the clock, while smoking. Wrapping the brisket in aluminum foil cuts down on smoking time and prevents the meat from drying out.

PREP TIME **2 DAYS**	COOK TIME **1–2 HRS**	SERVES **8**	HEAT **INDIRECT 225°F (107°C)**	COOKING SURFACE **STANDARD GRATE**

Curing and smoking beef tenderloin yields deeply flavored, succulent meat. Serve thinly sliced on hoagie rolls along with the Dijon mustard cream sauce.

SMOKED BEEF TENDERLOIN
with mustard cream sauce

INGREDIENTS

1 whole beef tenderloin, about 5lb (2.3kg) in total, trimmed

¼ cup extra virgin olive oil

kosher salt and freshly ground black pepper

4 garlic cloves, minced

¼ cup chopped fresh basil

¼ cup chopped fresh rosemary

¼ cup chopped fresh oregano

¼ cup chopped fresh marjoram

¼ cup chopped fresh flat-leaf parsley

8 hoagie rolls, to serve

for the sauce

2 tbsp mustard seeds

¼ cup Dijon mustard

¼ cup whole grain mustard

5 tbsp mayonnaise

5 tbsp sour cream

2¼ tsp Worcestershire sauce

to smoke

alder, hickory, or apricot wood chunks

METHOD

1 Rub beef with oil, salt, pepper, garlic, basil, rosemary, oregano, marjoram, and parsley. Wrap tightly with plastic wrap and refrigerate for 4 to 24 hours.

2 To make the sauce, in a medium bowl, combine mustard seeds, Dijon mustard, whole grain mustard, mayonnaise, sour cream, and Worcestershire sauce. Cover the bowl and refrigerate for 1 hour or overnight to allow the flavors to meld.

3 Preheat the grill to 225°F (107°C). Once hot, add the wood chunks and install the heat deflector and a standard grate. Place tenderloin on the grate, close the lid, and smoke until the internal temperature reaches 125°F (52°C), about 1 to 2 hours.

4 Transfer beef to a cutting board and let rest for 15 minutes. While the meat rests, place rolls on the grate cut side down and lightly toast, about 2 to 3 minutes. Thinly slice the meat. To serve, spread the mustard cream sauce on the rolls and pile on the beef.

 TIP You can also slice the beef into thick steaks, coat with the mustard cream, and sear in a hot cast iron skillet until an evenly brown crust forms, about 2 to 3 minutes per side.

PREP TIME
30 MINS

COOK TIME
15 MINS

SERVES
12

HEAT
DIRECT
400°F (204°C)

COOKING SURFACE
CAST IRON GRATE

This twist on the traditional slider features the juiciness of ground beef paired with the distinct flavor of lamb. The tangy cornichon and caper sauce adds a little zing.

BEEF & LAMB SLIDERS
with cornichon & caper sauce

INGREDIENTS

1½lb (450g) 80% lean ground beef

1lb (680g) ground lamb

kosher salt and freshly ground black pepper

1 tbsp dried marjoram

for the sauce

6 cornichon pickles, coarsely chopped

4 tbsp coarsely chopped fresh flat-leaf parsley

1 tbsp drained capers

4 garlic cloves, peeled

1 tsp ground cayenne pepper

½ cup mayonnaise

2 tbsp whole grain mustard

to serve

12 slider buns

4oz (110g) paneer cheese, cut into 12 thick slices

2 large Roma tomatoes, thickly sliced

METHOD

1 To make the sauce, in a food processor, place cornichons, parsley, capers, and garlic, and pulse until finely chopped. Add cayenne, mayonnaise, and mustard, and pulse until blended.

2 In a large bowl, gently combine beef and lamb, and season well with salt and pepper. Add 2 tbsp of the cornichon and caper sauce to the meat, and gently mix. Form the mixture into 12 equally sized patties and make a slight indentation in the center of each with your thumb.

3 Preheat the grill to 400°F (204°C) using direct heat with a cast iron grate installed. Place the bun halves on the grate cut side down and grill for 1 minute. Transfer buns, cut side up, to a work surface, and spread the bottom half of each bun with a spoonful of the remaining cornichon and caper sauce.

4 Place the patties on the grate, close the lid, and grill until charred on the bottom, about 4 minutes. Flip the sliders and grill until the internal temperature reaches 155°F (68°C), about 4 minutes more. Transfer the burgers to the toasted buns and let rest for 5 minutes.

5 Place the paneer slices on the grate and grill until soft, about 2 minutes per side. Top the sliders with grilled paneer and sliced tomatoes. Serve immediately.

PREP TIME
30 MINS

COOK TIME
70-80 MINS

SERVES
4

HEAT
INDIRECT
225°F (107°C)

COOKING SURFACE
CAST IRON SKILLET
STANDARD GRATE
CAST IRON GRATE

This steak is first smoked and then seared, resulting in tender meat with a beautifully browned exterior. The acidity and spice of the accompanying romesco sauce balance the richness of the meat.

REVERSE-SEAR RIBEYE
with spicy romesco sauce

INGREDIENTS

2lb (1kg) ribeye steak

1 tbsp vegetable oil

kosher salt and freshly ground black pepper

for the sauce

3 red bell peppers, left whole

½ bunch of scallions, trimmed

⅓ cup whole almonds

3 large garlic cloves

½ tsp crushed red pepper flakes

2 tbsp lemon juice

½ tsp kosher salt

¼ cup extra virgin olive oil

to smoke

pecan or bourbon barrel wood chunks

METHOD

1 Preheat the grill to 225°F (107°C). Once hot, add the wood chunks and install the heat deflector and a standard grate with a cast iron skillet on the grate.

2 In the hot skillet, place almonds and toast until golden brown, about 10 to 15 minutes, stirring occasionally. Remove the skillet from the grill and set aside.

3 Rub steak with oil, season with salt and pepper to taste, and place on the grate. Smoke until the internal temperature reaches 115°F (46°C), about 30 minutes per pound (approximately 1 hour per kilogram). Transfer to a platter and set aside.

4 Remove the heat deflector, replace the standard grate with a cast iron grate, and open the top and bottom vents to raise the grill temperature to 500°F (260°C) using direct heat. Place peppers and scallions on the grate, and grill until beginning to soften and char, about 3 minutes per side, turning once. Remove from the grill, seed and roughly chop the peppers, and roughly chop the scallions.

5 To make the sauce, in a food processor, combine almonds, garlic, and red pepper flakes, and pulse until finely ground. Add peppers, scallions, lemon juice, and salt, and purée, adding oil in a slow stream. Season with black pepper to taste.

6 Place steak on the grate and sear until steak reaches your desired level of doneness, about 2 to 3 minutes per side for medium rare. Transfer to a cutting board and thinly slice. Top with the romesco sauce, and serve immediately.

PREP TIME
4–24 HRS

COOK TIME
3½ HRS

SERVES
8

HEAT
**INDIRECT
350ºF (177ºC)**

COOKING SURFACE
**CAST IRON GRATE
DUTCH OVEN**

This spice-rubbed steak is first smoked and then braised with aromatics in wine and broth, resulting in deliciously tender meat that's permeated with flavor and a rich broth for serving.

SMOKED & BRAISED BEEF CHUCK STEAK

INGREDIENTS

2½lb (1.2kg) thick-cut chuck steak

1 large yellow onion, halved

1 green bell pepper, halved

4 tbsp extra virgin olive oil

4 garlic cloves, smashed

4 carrots, cut into ½-in
  (1.25-cm) pieces

3 celery stalks, cut into 1-in
  (2.5-cm) pieces

peels of 2 oranges, thinly sliced

½ cup fruity red wine

2½ cups beef or chicken stock

kosher salt and freshly ground
  black pepper

for the rub

¼ cup kosher salt

4 tbsp ground black pepper

2 tbsp garlic salt

1 tbsp paprika

1 tbsp ground cayenne pepper

¼ cup raw sugar

to smoke

post oak, wine barrel, or grapevine
  wood chunks

METHOD

1 To make the rub, in a small bowl, combine all the rub ingredients. Rub spice mixture all over steak to ensure even and full coverage. Wrap tightly with plastic wrap and refrigerate for 4 to 24 hours. Before smoking, remove steak from the fridge and allow to come to room temperature.

2 Preheat the grill to 350°F (177°C). Once hot, add the wood chunks and install the heat deflector and a drip pan. Install a cast iron grate with a Dutch oven on the grate. Place onion and pepper on the grate, close the lid, and grill until beginning to soften and char, about 7 to 10 minutes. Transfer onion and pepper to a cutting board and thinly slice. Set aside.

3 Place steak on the grate, close the lid, and smoke until the internal temperature reaches 190°F (88°C), about 45 minutes. Remove steak from the grill and let rest for 10 to 15 minutes. (Cut into large pieces for braising if needed.)

4 To braise the meat, heat oil in the Dutch oven until shimmering. Add the smoked steak and the grilled onion and pepper to the Dutch oven along with garlic, carrots, celery, orange peels, wine, and stock. (Steak should be fully submerged in liquid). Leaving the Dutch oven uncovered, close the grill lid and cook until steak is tender, about 2½ hours, turning once halfway through.

5 Transfer steak to a cutting board, thickly slice across the grain, and arrange on a large serving platter along with some of the braised vegetables. Skim any fat from the braising liquid and spoon some of the liquid over the steak and vegetables. Season with salt and pepper to taste. Serve immediately.

PREP TIME
30 MINS

COOK TIME
3 HRS

SERVES
10

HEAT
INDIRECT
325°F (163°C)

COOKING SURFACE
DUTCH OVEN

In traditional northwoods style, this chili is heavy on beans and vegetables and fiery spices. A low, slow simmer over maple wood allows the flavors to meld and infuses the chili with smoke.

SMOKED CANUCK CHILI

INGREDIENTS

2lb (1kg) lean ground beef

½ large yellow onion, diced

3 tbsp garlic powder

1 tbsp seasoned pepper

2 tbsp crushed red pepper flakes, plus more to taste

2 x 4oz (133g) cans mushroom pieces, drained

28oz (794g) can baked beans

2 x 15oz (425g) cans kidney beans, with liquid

2 x 6oz (150g) cans tomato paste

¼ cup sugar

3 medium carrots, diced

3 celery stalks, diced

1 red bell pepper, diced

2 jalapeño peppers, diced

¼ cup lager beer

¼ cup BBQ sauce

2 tsp hot sauce, plus more to taste

to smoke

maple or alder wood chunks

METHOD

1 Preheat the grill to 325°F (163°C) using indirect heat with a Dutch oven on the heat deflector. To the hot Dutch oven, add beef, onion, garlic powder, seasoned pepper, and red pepper flakes. Close the lid and cook until the meat has browned, about 5 to 10 minutes. Remove the Dutch oven and heat deflector, drain off the fat, and add wood chunks to the coals.

2 Reinstall the heat deflector and replace the Dutch oven. Add mushrooms, baked beans, kidney beans with liquid, tomato paste, sugar, carrots, celery, pepper, jalapeños, beer, BBQ sauce, and hot sauce to the Dutch oven. Stir to combine, and season with more red pepper flakes and hot sauce to taste.

3 Close the top and bottom vents most of the way to lower the grill temperature to 225°F (107°C). Leaving the Dutch oven uncovered, close the grill lid, and smoke for 2 to 3 hours.

4 Remove the Dutch oven from the grill, and serve immediately.

TIP Use seasonal vegetables—along with those already in this dish or in place of them—to make variations of this recipe throughout the year.

PREP TIME
30 MINS

COOK TIME
20–30 MINS

MAKES
4 BURGERS

HEAT
**INDIRECT
400ºF (163ºC)**

COOKING SURFACE
CAST IRON GRATE

A beer can is used to shape these stuffed burgers, which are loaded with grilled onions, BBQ sauce, and relish. The addition of wild rice to the meat mixture makes a substantial and satisfying patty.

BEER CAN BBQ BURGERS

INGREDIENTS

½ medium white onion

2lb (1kg) ground chuck

¼ cup cooked wild rice

3 tbsp sweet paprika

2 tbsp Dijon mustard

2 tbsp minced garlic

2 tbsp kosher salt, plus more as needed

2 tbsp ground black pepper, plus more as needed

9 tbsp smoky BBQ sauce, divided

4 tbsp sweet pepper relish

4 tbsp prepared horseradish

4 hamburger buns

to serve

lettuce leaves

tomato slices

onion slices

METHOD

1 Preheat the grill to 400 °F (163°C) using indirect heat with a cast iron grate installed. Place onion on the grate, close the lid, and grill until beginning to soften and char, about 7 to 10 minutes. Remove onion from the grill and dice. Set aside.

2 In a large bowl, use your hands to combine beef, cooked rice, paprika, mustard, garlic, salt, pepper, and 1 tbsp BBQ sauce. Form the mixture into 4 patties, and press a can of beer or soda into the middle of each patty to create an indentation. Season the patties with salt and pepper, and fill the indentations with the grilled onion and relish, evenly dividing the filling ingredients among the 4 patties. Top each burger with 1 tbsp BBQ sauce.

3 Place the patties on the grate, close the lid, and grill until the internal temperature reaches 155°F (68°C), about 8 to 12 minutes. Don't move or flip the burgers.

4 In a small bowl, combine horseradish and remaining 4 tbsp BBQ sauce. Remove the burgers from the grill and let rest for a few minutes. While the burgers rest, place the bun halves cut side down on the grate and toast for 3 to 5 minutes.

5 Spread the bottom buns with the BBQ horseradish mixture. Place a patty on each bottom bun, top with lettuce, tomato, and onion, and place the top buns. Serve immediately.

PREP TIME
1 HR

COOK TIME
35 MINS

SERVES
4

HEAT
DIRECT
450°F (232°C)

COOKING SURFACE
STANDARD GRATE
CAST IRON SKILLET

Thin strips of tender beef are marinated in a sweet and savory sauce, then tossed with grilled carrots, peppers, peas, and scallions. Hazelnuts add a nutty flavor and pleasing crunch.

HAZELNUT BEEF STIR-FRY
with honey-soy sauce

INGREDIENTS

¾ cup hazelnuts

2 carrots, peeled

1 tbsp sesame oil

1lb (450g) top round steak, cut into thin strips

1 green bell pepper, cut into ¾-in (2-cm) slices

4oz sugar snap peas, trimmed and cut into bite-sized pieces

6 scallions, cut into 2-in (5-cm) sections, plus more to garnish

2 cups cooked white rice, to serve

for the marinade

⅔ cup honey

2 tbsp soy sauce

2 tbsp sherry

1 tbsp sesame oil

½ tsp ground mustard

¼ tsp garlic powder

¼ tsp ground ginger

2 tsp cornstarch

METHOD

1 To make the marinade, in a medium bowl, combine all the marinade ingredients. Place beef in a resealable plastic bag, pour in the marinade, and refrigerate for 30 minutes.

2 Preheat the grill to 450°F (232°C) using direct heat with a standard grate installed and a cast iron skillet on the grate.

3 In the hot skillet, place hazelnuts and toast until beginning to brown, about 4 to 6 minutes. Remove hazelnuts from the skillet, roughly chop, and set aside. Clean the skillet and return it to the grate to return to temperature.

4 Place carrots on the grate, close the lid, and grill until beginning to soften and char, about 7 to 10 minutes. Remove from the grill and slice into thin rounds.

5 In the hot skillet, heat oil until shimmering. Add beef to the skillet, reserving the marinade. Add carrots, pepper, peas, scallions, and half the hazelnuts to the skillet. Cook until the meat is cooked through and the vegetables are tender and crisp, about 7 minutes, stirring once or twice.

6 Add the reserved marinade to the skillet and bring to a simmer. Cook until thickened, about 10 minutes, stirring once or twice. Transfer the stir-fry to a serving dish, sprinkle the remaining hazelnuts and some sliced scallions over top, and serve immediately with rice.

PREP TIME
6-9 DAYS

COOK TIME
12 HRS

SERVES
16

HEAT
INDIRECT
225°F (107°C)

COOKING SURFACE
STANDARD GRATE

This cured, smoked beef is tender and deeply flavored thanks to a long soak in a savory brine. Serve thinly sliced on a hoagie roll with your choice of cheese and toppings—and a pickle on the side.

HOMEMADE PASTRAMI

INGREDIENTS

15lb (6.8kg) beef brisket

for the brine

1 cup kosher salt

1 gallon (3.8 liters) water

2 tsp ground coriander

1 cup packed dark brown sugar

2 tsp pink curing salt

1 tsp ground juniper berries

½ tsp ground ginger

½ tsp granulated garlic

½ tsp ground cloves

for the rub

½ cup coarse ground black pepper

¼ cup ground coriander

2 tsp mustard powder

2 tbsp light brown sugar

2 tbsp paprika

4 tsp garlic powder

4 tsp onion powder

to smoke

hickory, oak, or apple, wood chunks

METHOD

1 In a stockpot or other large vessel, combine all the brine ingredients and bring to a boil on the stovetop over high heat. Remove the vessel from the heat and refrigerate to allow to cool completely. (Any extra brine can be refrigerated and saved for a later use.) Once the brine has cooled, submerge brisket in the brine, cover with plastic wrap, and refrigerate for 5 to 8 days.

2 Remove brisket from the curing liquid and pat dry with paper towels. In a small bowl, combine all the rub ingredients. Thoroughly coat brisket on all sides with the rub. Wrap tightly in plastic wrap and refrigerate for 24 hours.

3 Preheat the grill to 225°F (107°C). Once hot, add the wood chunks and install the heat deflector and a standard grate. Place brisket on the grate and smoke until the internal temperature reaches 185°F (85°C), about 12 hours.

4 Remove brisket from the grill and let rest for 30 minutes before slicing and serving.

 TIP Be sure to use pink curing salt, not pink seasoning salt, in the brine. Curing salt, such as Insta Cure, is intended for food preservation and helps to inhibit bacteria growth during the long brine.

PREP TIME
24 HRS

COOK TIME
3 HRS

SERVES
6

HEAT
INDIRECT
275°F (135°C)

COOKING SURFACE
STANDARD GRATE

Chuck roast is a relatively inexpensive cut that benefits from low, slow cooking to break down the connective tissue. Top with a BBQ sauce that offers more than just a tangy kick.

PULLED BEEF SANDWICH
with spicy mustard BBQ sauce

INGREDIENTS

3lb (1.4kg) boneless chuck roast

for the rub

¼ cup packed light brown sugar

3 tbsp kosher salt

3 tbsp ground black pepper

2 tbsp garlic powder

for the sauce

¼ cup BBQ sauce

2 cups ketchup

2 tbsp gochujang

3 tbsp Worcestershire sauce

3 tbsp Dijon mustard

1 tbsp kosher salt

¼ tbsp ground black pepper

to serve

6 sandwich buns, split

sliced onions

dill pickles

pickled hot peppers

to smoke

hickory wood chunks

METHOD

1 To make the rub, in a small bowl, combine sugar, salt, pepper, and garlic powder. Evenly coat roast with the rub, wrap tightly with plastic wrap, and refrigerate for 24 hours. Remove roast from the fridge and allow to come to room temperature.

2 Preheat the grill to 275°F (135°C). Once hot, add the wood chunks and install the heat deflector and a standard grate. Place roast on the grate, close the lid, and smoke until the internal temperature reaches 165°F (74°C), about 60 to 90 minutes.

3 To make the sauce, in a small bowl, combine BBQ sauce, ketchup, gochujang, Worcestershire sauce, mustard, salt, and pepper. Shape some aluminum foil into a bowl, remove roast from the grill, and place roast in the foil bowl. Coat roast with the sauce, allowing the excess to pool in the foil, and wrap roast tightly to prevent sauce or steam from escaping.

4 Return foil-wrapped roast to the grill, close the lid, and smoke until the internal temperature reaches 185°F (85°C) and the meat shreds easily, about 60 to 90 minutes. Transfer the roast to a large serving platter and let rest 30 minutes, keeping it wrapped in the foil.

5 Unwrap roast, shred with two forks, and pour the sauce from the foil over top. Serve immediately on buns, topping with onions, pickles, and hot peppers or other desired toppings.

PREP TIME
30 MINS

COOK TIME
45–70 MINUTES

SERVES
8

HEAT
**INDIRECT
400°F (204°C)**

COOKING SURFACE
**CAST IRON GRATE
CAST IRON SKILLET**

This bacon-wrapped meatloaf is cooked on the grill, then sliced and grilled again for an impressive presentation and robust flavor. A scoop of tangy tomato relish completes the dish.

GRILLED MEATLOAF
with tomato relish

INGREDIENTS

2lb (1kg) ground chuck

1lb (450g) ground pork

1 cup panko breadcrumbs

2 large eggs

2 sprigs of fresh thyme, leaves only

kosher salt and freshly ground black pepper

8 bacon slices (not thick cut)

olive oil

for the relish

1 medium white onion, halved

3 red bell peppers, halved

2 tbsp extra virgin olive oil

3 garlic cloves, minced

3 bay leaves

3 tomatoes, seeded and finely diced

1/3 cup chopped fresh flat-leaf parsley

1 cup ketchup

4½ tsp Worcestershire sauce

kosher salt and freshly ground black pepper

METHOD

1 Preheat the grill to 400°F (204°C) using indirect heat with a cast iron grate and a cast iron skillet installed. Place onion and peppers on the grate (not in the skillet) and grill until beginning to soften and char, about 7 to 10 minutes. Remove the vegetables from the grill, dice the onion, and seed and dice the peppers.

2 To make the relish, in the hot skillet, heat oil until shimmering. Add onion, garlic, and bay leaves, and sauté for 2 to 3 minutes. Add peppers, and sauté for 2 to 3 minutes more, then add the tomatoes. Stir in parsley, ketchup, and Worcestershire sauce. Season with salt and pepper to taste. Simmer for 3 minutes, remove bay leaves, and remove the skillet from the grill. (You should have about 2 cups of relish.)

3 In a large bowl, combine ground beef, ground pork, breadcrumbs, eggs, thyme, and ½ cup relish. Season salt and pepper to taste. Form the meat mixture into a 9 x 4in (23 x 10cm) loaf. Lay bacon slices flat on a work surface, overlapping the long edges slightly to form a rectangle. Place the meatloaf crosswise on the bacon and bring the ends of the bacon strips up and around the meat so the meatloaf is fully wrapped in bacon.

4 Place the meatloaf seam side down in the center of the grill, close the lid, and grill until the internal temperature reaches 160°F (71°C), about 30 to 45 minutes. Transfer the meatloaf to a serving platter and let cool completely.

5 Cut the cooled meatloaf into thick slices. Brush a small amount of oil on both sides of each slice, return to the grill, close the lid, and grill for 2 to 3 minutes per side. Serve immediately with the remaining relish, warmed on the stovetop (if desired).

PREP TIME
30 MINS

COOK TIME
8 MINS

SERVES
16

HEAT
DIRECT
400°F (204°C)

COOKING SURFACE
CAST IRON GRIDDLE

Smashing patties into grilling shallots gives the burgers instant flavor as they sizzle and steam. This makes the burgers more compact, helping retain the caramelized taste of the shallots.

SMASH BURGERS

INGREDIENTS

2 tbsp unsalted butter

2 tbsp canola oil

½ cup minced shallots or red onion

2lb (1kg) ground chuck

kosher salt and freshly ground black pepper

16 sweet Hawaiian rolls or slider buns

5oz (140g) Brie or cheese of choice, cut into 16 slices

tomato slices, to serve

dill pickle slices, to serve

METHOD

1 Preheat the grill to 400°F (204°C) using direct heat with a cast iron grate installed flat side up. To the hot griddle, add butter and canola oil. Make 8 small piles of half the shallots on the griddle, about 2 tsp per pile.

2 Portion ground beef into 16 balls, and season with salt and pepper to taste. Place one meatball on each pile of shallots. Using a spatula, smash the meat into the shallots, forming a thin patty.

3 Close the lid and grill the burgers until shallots begin to caramelize and the meat is cooked on the bottom, about 2 minutes. Don't move the patties. When the bottoms are caramelized, flip the burgers, being sure to get most of the shallots.

4 Place a slice of cheese on each patty and the top bun on the cheese. Leave in place on the griddle for 2 minutes. On a serving platter, top the bottom halves of the buns with tomato and pickle slices. Using a spatula, slide the burgers and top buns from the griddle and place atop the bottom buns. Repeat steps 2 through 4 with the remaining shallots, meat, and toppings. Serve immediately.

TIP You can replace the shallots with any kind of onion, especially red onions, which offer a similar texture and flavor to the burgers. You can also add other toppings to your burgers as desired.

PREP TIME
30 MINS

COOK TIME
30 MINS

MAKES
12 MEATBALLS

HEAT
**INDIRECT
375°F (191°C)**

COOKING SURFACE
**STANDARD GRATE
CAST IRON SKILLET**

These meatballs are great with your favorite pasta or on their own. The capers enrich the tomato sauce, highlighting its pungency. Serve with crusty bread and a garden salad for a complete meal.

ITALIAN MEATBALLS
in caper & tomato sauce

INGREDIENTS

¼ cup panko breadcrumbs, lightly toasted

¾lb (340g) Roma tomatoes, peeled and chopped

2 tbsp extra virgin olive oil, divided

½ tbsp nonpareil capers, drained and chopped

½ tsp dried oregano

½ tsp dried marjoram

1 tbsp fresh basil, plus more for serving, chopped

⅓lb (150g) ground pork

⅓lb (150g) ground beef

⅓lb (150g) ground veal

3 tsp whole milk

1 large egg, lightly beaten

2 pitted Kalamata olives, minced

1 tbsp grated Parmesan cheese, plus more for serving

1 tbsp fresh flat-leaf parsley, minced

1 tsp kosher salt, plus more as needed

freshly ground black pepper

METHOD

1 Preheat the grill to 375°F (191°C) using indirect heat with a standard grate and a cast iron skillet installed.

2 On a rimmed sheet pan, place breadcrumbs in a single layer and toast until beginning to brown, about 3 to 5 minutes. Remove the pan from the grill and set aside.

3 Place tomatoes in a food processor and purée. Place tomatoes and 1 tbsp oil in the skillet. Bring to a boil, slightly close the top and bottom vents to reduce the temperature to 325°F (163°C), close the lid, and simmer until the sauce starts to thicken, about 5 minutes, stirring occasionally.

4 Add capers, oregano, and marjoram to the skillet, and simmer until the sauce has reduced to 1¼ cups, about 5 minutes. Add basil, season with salt to taste, and set aside.

5 In a large bowl, combine pork, beef, and veal. Add breadcrumbs, milk, egg, olives, Parmesan cheese, parsley, and salt, and mix well with your hands. Shape the mixture into 12 meatballs.

6 Slightly open the top and bottom vents to return the temperature to 375°F (191°C). Once the grill reaches the needed temperature, return the skillet to the grill and heat the remaining 1 tbsp oil until shimmering. Place the meatballs in the skillet, close the lid, and cook until they start to brown, about 8 minutes, turning once every 2 minutes. Add the sauce, close the lid, and cook until the meatballs are cooked through and the sauce is hot, about 8 minutes.

7 Remove the meatballs from the grill, place on a large serving platter, and top with more Parmesan cheese and basil. Serve immediately.

PREP TIME
24 HRS

COOK TIME
4 HRS

SERVES
8

HEAT
**INDIRECT
325ºF (163ºC)**

COOKING SURFACE
**DUTCH OVEN
STANDARD GRATE**

These slow-cooked short ribs are moist, tender, and generously coated with a robust BBQ sauce. The sweet cherries in the sauce are balanced by the coffee-like bitterness of stout and molasses.

BEEF SHORT RIBS
with cherry-stout BBQ sauce

INGREDIENTS

2 racks of beef short ribs, about 6lb (2.7kg) in total

kosher salt and freshly ground black pepper

for the sauce

2 cups frozen dark sweet cherries

1 cup ketchup

2 cups stout or other dark beer

¾ cup molasses

½ cup packed light brown sugar

1 tbsp mustard powder

1 tbsp chipotle powder

1 tbsp paprika

1 tbsp chili powder

1 tbsp onion powder

to smoke

cherry, hickory, or oak wood chunks

METHOD

1 Season ribs well on all sides with salt and pepper. Wrap tightly in plastic wrap and refrigerate overnight.

2 Preheat the grill to 325°F (163°C). Once hot, add the wood chunks, install the heat deflector, and place a Dutch oven on the heat deflector.

3 To make the sauce, add the cherries to the hot Dutch oven and cook for 5 minutes. Stir in the remaining sauce ingredients and cook until the mixture has reduced by one-fourth, about 25 minutes. Season with salt and pepper to taste, and remove the Dutch oven from the grill.

4 Remove the ribs from the fridge and bring to room temperature. After removing the Dutch oven from the grill, place a drip pan on the heat deflector and install a standard grate. Place ribs flat on the grate and close the grill lid. Smoke until the meat is tender and the internal temperature reaches 190°F (88°C), about 3 hours.

5 Once ribs have come to temperature, brush with the sauce and smoke until the ribs are well coated, about 10 minutes more, continuing to brush with sauce every few minutes. Serve immediately with any remaining sauce.

PREP TIME
4-24 HRS

COOK TIME
30-45 MINS

SERVES
16

HEAT
**DIRECT
525°F (274°C)**

COOKING SURFACE
CAST IRON GRATE

An overnight marinade in citrus juices and chipotle peppers infuses this flank steak with flavor. Serve thinly sliced in warm tortillas along with grilled vegetables, cheese, and sour cream.

FLANK STEAK FAJITAS
with grilled vegetables

INGREDIENTS

4½lb (2kg) flank steak, trimmed and cut into 8-in (20-cm) pieces

2 red bell peppers, halved and seeded

2 green bell peppers, halved and seeded

2 large white onions, halved

4 radishes, halved

4 tbsp olive oil

kosher salt and freshly ground black pepper

juice of 4 limes

3 large tomatoes, diced

¼ cup chopped fresh cilantro

for the marinade

juice of 4 limes

juice of 2 oranges

½ cup vegetable oil

4 garlic cloves, roughly chopped

7oz (199g) chipotle peppers in adobo, with sauce

½ cup roughly chopped fresh cilantro

2 tsp ground cumin

2 tsp salt

to serve

32 x 8-in (20-cm) flour tortillas

4 avocados, sliced

sour cream

queso Chihuahua (soft Mexican cheese), shredded

METHOD

1 To make the marinade, in a food processor, combine all the marinade ingredients, and pulse until smooth. Divide the marinade between 2 resealable plastic bags, add steak pieces, and thoroughly coat. Squeeze out any excess air and refrigerate for 4 to 24 hours. Before grilling, remove steak from the marinade, pat dry with paper towels, and allow to come to room temperature.

2 Preheat the grill to 525°F (274°C) using direct heat with a cast iron grate installed. In a large bowl, toss peppers, onions, and radishes with olive oil, and season liberally with salt and pepper. Place the vegetables on the grate, close the lid, and grill until beginning to soften and char, about 7 to 10 minutes. Remove the vegetables from the grill and set aside.

3 Place steak pieces on the grate, close the lid, and grill until distinct grill marks appear and the internal temperature reaches 130°F (54°C), about 4 to 6 minutes per side. Remove steak from the grill and let rest for 5 minutes.

4 Thinly slice the grilled peppers, onions, and radishes. In a large bowl, toss the vegetables with lime juice, tomatoes, and cilantro, and season with salt and pepper to taste. Thinly slice steak against the grain on the diagonal.

5 Place 8 tortillas on the grate, close the lid, and grill until grill marks begin to appear, about 1 to 2 minutes per side. Remove from the grill and place on individual serving platters. Repeat this step with the remaining tortillas.

6 To assemble the fajitas, fill the tortillas with steak slices and grilled vegetables, and top with avocado, sour cream, and queso. Serve immediately.

PREP TIME
4–24 HRS

COOK TIME
2 HRS

SERVES
6

HEAT
INDIRECT
275ºF (135ºC)

COOKING SURFACE
STANDARD GRATE

Zhug is a Middle Eastern hot sauce that in this recipe is made with gochujang, a paste made from hot peppers, as well as poblano peppers—a combination sure to enhance the loin's rich flavor.

SMOKED STRIP LOIN
with spicy gochujang zhug

INGREDIENTS

6lb (2.7kg) New York strip loin

for the zhug

8 garlic cloves, peeled

5 poblano pepper, left whole

½ cup chopped fresh cilantro

2 tbsp lemon juice

1 tbsp ground coriander

1 tbsp ground cardamom

1 tbsp kosher salt

½ cup chopped fresh flat-leaf parsley

4 tbsp gochujang paste, divided

¾ cup canola oil, plus more as needed

to smoke

apple, hickory, or apricot wood chunks

METHOD

1 Preheat the grill to 275°F (135°C). Once hot, add the wood chunks and install the heat deflector and a standard grate. Wrap garlic in aluminum foil, place garlic and poblanos on the grate, close the lid, and cook until beginning to soften and char, about 15 to 20 minutes.

2 To make the zhug, in a food processor, combine garlic, poblanos, cilantro, lemon juice, coriander, cardamom, salt, parsley, and 2 tbsp gochujang. Pulse until a coarse paste forms. Reserve ¼ cup zhug and set aside. Transfer the remaining zhug to an airtight container, stir in oil, and refrigerate until ready to use.

3 In a small bowl, combine reserved ¼ cup zhug and the remaining 2 tbsp gochujang, and add just enough oil to fully combine. Rub loin with the mixture, wrap tightly in plastic wrap, and refrigerate for at least 4 hours or overnight.

4 Remove loin from the fridge and allow to come to room temperature. Place loin on the grate, close the lid, and smoke until the internal temperature reaches 120°F (49°C), about 90 minutes. Remove loin from the grill and place on a baking pan.

5 Slightly close the top and bottom vents to raise the temperature to 500°F (260°C), top loin with half the refrigerated zhug, and place the pan on the grate. Close the lid and cook until the internal temperature reaches 130°F (54°C), about 8 to 10 minutes.

6 Remove loin from the grill and let rest for 20 minutes. Slice and serve with the remaining zhug, adjusting the seasoning as needed.

PREP TIME	COOK TIME	SERVES	HEAT	COOKING SURFACE
24 HRS	**2 HRS**	**8**	**INDIRECT** **225°F (107°C)**	**STANDARD GRATE**

Few things are more impressive and celebratory than freshly carved prime rib. Juicy and deeply flavorful, this aged beef is smoked and served with decadent marrow butter and savory jus.

AGED PRIME RIB
with marrow butter

INGREDIENTS

2 tsp garlic salt

2 tsp onion salt

2 tsp kosher salt

1 tsp freshly ground black pepper

2 tsp dried rosemary

4lb (1.8kg) bone-in prime rib roast, aged for at least 28 days

3 garlic cloves, slivered

½ to 1 cup beef stock, as needed

for the marrow butter

2 beef marrow bones, cut in half lengthwise at the butcher

½lb (225g) butter, softened

¾ tsp chopped fresh flat-leaf parsley

kosher salt and freshly ground black pepper

to smoke

hickory or oak wood chunks

METHOD

1 In a medium bowl, combine garlic salt, onion salt, kosher salt, pepper, and rosemary. Place roast in a baking dish and use a sharp knife to cut tiny slits every 2 inches (5cm), and insert the garlic slivers in the slits. Rub the roast with the spice mixture, cover with plastic wrap, and refrigerate for 24 hours.

2 Preheat the grill to 225°F (107°C). Once hot, add the wood chunks, install the heat deflector with a drip pan placed on top, and install a standard grate. Place roast and marrow bones on the grate, close the lid, and smoke until the internal temperature of the meat reaches 125°F (52°C), about 2 hours. Transfer roast to a large platter, cover with aluminum foil, and set aside to rest.

3 Remove the bones from the grill, and use a spoon to scrape the marrow from the bones into a medium bowl. To make the marrow butter, add butter and parsley to the marrow, and mix until well combined. Season with salt and pepper to taste. Set aside.

4 Remove the drip pan from the grill and pour the drippings into a medium all-metal saucepan. Place the saucepan on the heat deflector, close the lid, and heat for 10 minutes, adding beef stock as needed. Season with salt and pepper to taste.

5 Place roast on a cutting board and slice. Serve immediately with the marrow butter and warm jus for dipping.

PORK

A long, slow smoke and a tangy malt vinegar mop sauce infuse this pulled pork with flavor. Piled high on soft sandwich buns and topped with creamy coleslaw, it's perfect for your next BBQ.

CAROLINA PULLED PORK
with creamy coleslaw

INGREDIENTS

10lb (4.5kg) boneless pork shoulder

20 sandwich buns, to serve

for the rub

4 tbsp paprika

2 tbsp ground black pepper

4 tsp ground cayenne pepper

for the coleslaw

½ cup mayonnaise

3 tbsp apple cider vinegar

1 tbsp sugar

1 tbsp celery seed

1 head of napa cabbage, shredded

2 large carrots, shredded

for the sauce

1 cup bourbon

4 tbsp molasses

3 cups malt vinegar

2 cups water

4 dried chipotle peppers, rehydrated and chopped

4 tbsp kosher salt

2 tbsp crushed red pepper flakes

2 tbsp ground black pepper

4 tsp ground cayenne pepper

to smoke

hickory or oak wood chunks

METHOD

1 To make the rub, in a small bowl, combine paprika, pepper, and cayenne. Place pork on a baking pan and rub the mixture over all surfaces. Cover with plastic wrap and refrigerate for 24 hours.

2 To make the coleslaw, in a large bowl, whisk together mayonnaise, vinegar, sugar, and celery seed until well combined. Add cabbage and carrots, and toss to coat. Cover with plastic wrap and refrigerate for at least 4 hours.

3 Preheat the grill to 275°F (135°C). Once hot, add the wood chunks and install the heat deflector and a standard grate. Place pork on a V-rack over a drip pan and place on the grate. Close the lid and smoke until the internal temperature reaches 190°F (88°C), about 6 to 8 hours.

4 To make the sauce, in a saucepan, combine all the sauce ingredients and place the pan on the stovetop over medium heat. Simmer for 5 minutes. During the last 2 hours of smoking, baste pork with the sauce every 20 to 30 minutes. Keep any sauce in the pan that remains after basting.

5 Transfer pork to a large platter to rest. Remove the drip pan and add the accumulated drippings to the saucepan with the remaining sauce. Heat on the stovetop over medium heat until warm, about 5 minutes.

6 Remove pork from the grill and shred, discarding any large pieces of fat and adding the sauce as desired. Pile pork on sandwich buns and top with coleslaw.

PREP TIME
1–3 DAYS

COOK TIME
4½ HRS

SERVES
16

HEAT
**INDIRECT
300°F (149°C)**

COOKING SURFACE
**STANDARD GRATE
V-RACK**

This centerpiece dish of rolled pork belly is slow roasted,
resulting in tender meat, crackling skin, and unparalleled flavor.
Smoky potatoes roasted in pork drippings complete the meal.

PORCHETTA
with roasted potatoes

INGREDIENTS

1 boneless, skin-on pork belly,
 about 8lb (3.6kg) in total

4 tbsp kosher salt

4 tbsp rice flour

4lb (1.8kg) unpeeled red potatoes,
 diced large

for the rub

2 tbsp kosher salt

2 tbsp ground black pepper

3 tbsp ground fennel seed

3 tbsp ground cumin

1 tbsp crushed red pepper flakes

3 tbsp chopped fresh thyme

12 garlic cloves, minced

to smoke

apple, hickory, or cherry
 wood chunks

METHOD

1 To make the rub, in a medium bowl, combine all the rub ingredients. Place pork belly skin side down on a large cutting board. Use your hands to rub the mixture deeply into the cracks and crevices of the belly meat (not the skin).

2 Roll pork belly into a tight log and set aside, seam side down. Using kitchen twine, cut lengths long enough to tie around pork and cut enough strings to space about 1 inch (2.5cm) apart. Lay them down along a cutting board, about 1 inch (2.5cm) apart each. Place the rolled pork seam side down on top of the strings. Working from the outermost strings toward the center, tie up pork tightly.

3 Combine salt and rice flour. Rub the flour mixture over the entire surface of porchetta. Wrap tightly with plastic wrap and refrigerate overnight or up to 3 days. Before smoking, remove from the fridge and let come to room temperature.

4 Preheat the grill to 300°F (149°C) using indirect heat with a standard grate installed. Once hot, add the wood chunks, place pork in a V-rack, and set the rack in a drip pan. Place pork setup in the grill, close the lid, and roast until the internal temperature reaches 160°F, about 2 hours, basting with drippings every half hour.

5 After 1 hour of cooking, add potatoes to the drip pan and stir to coat. Continue roasting until a knife or skewer inserted into pork encounters very little resistance (aside from the outer layer of skin), about 2 more hours. Close the top and bottom vents to increase the temperature to 500°F (260°C) and continue roasting until the skin is completely crisp and potatoes are tender, about 20 to 30 minutes.

6 Remove pork from the grill and place on a cutting board tented with aluminum foil to rest for 15 minutes. Remove potatoes from drip pan and drain any excess fat. Season with salt and pepper to taste. Using a very sharp knife, slice the porchetta into disks about ¾ inch (2cm) thick. Serve with roasted potatoes.

PREP TIME
1 HR

COOK TIME
20–25 MINS

SERVES
12

HEAT
DIRECT
425°F (218°C)

COOKING SURFACE
CAST IRON GRATE

These juicy, brined pork chops are brushed with a tangy sauce that marries the salty, earthy flavor of miso with sweet and tart apricots. Mustard powder and ginger add a hint of spice.

APRICOT & MISO PORK CHOPS

INGREDIENTS

5lb (2.3kg) pork loin, trimmed and cut into 1½-in (3.75-cm) pork chops

kosher salt and freshly ground black pepper

for the brine

½ cup kosher salt

½ cup packed light brown sugar

3 tbsp pickling spice

6 cups hot water

for the sauce

1 cup sugar

1 cup rice vinegar

1 tbsp minced fresh ginger

1 cup chopped dried apricots

¼ cup white miso paste

¼ cup ground mustard powder

½ cup hot water

1 tsp fresh lemon juice

METHOD

1 To make the brine, in a large bowl, whisk together salt, brown sugar, pickling spice, and hot water until salt and sugar have dissolved. Add ice cubes a few at a time until the liquid is no longer hot. Place pork chops in 2 large resealable bags, add brine to cover, and refrigerate for 1 hour. (Any extra brine can be refrigerated and saved for a later use.)

2 To make the sauce, on the stovetop in a saucepan over high heat, combine sugar, vinegar, and ginger, and bring to a boil. Add apricots, lower the heat to medium, and simmer until soft, about 15 minutes. In a small bowl, combine miso, mustard powder, and hot water, and whisk until miso and mustard dissolve. Add miso mixture to the saucepan and simmer for 5 minutes. Transfer the sauce to a blender, add lemon juice, and blend until smooth. Reserve half the sauce and set aside.

3 Remove pork chops from the brine, pat dry with paper towels, and season with salt and pepper. Coat the chops liberally with miso sauce, and allow to come to room temperature.

4 Preheat the grill to 425°F (218°C) using direct heat with a cast iron grate installed. Place chops on the grate, close the lid, and grill until the internal temperature reaches 140°F (60°C), about 3 to 5 minutes per side, basting with the sauce and turning once.

5 Transfer the chops to a serving dish and spoon the reserved sauce over top. Tent with foil and let rest for 5 minutes before serving.

 To use fresh apricots in place of dried apricots, cut the ripe fruit into thick slices and grill until beginning to soften and char, about 7 to 10 minutes. Dice and use as directed.

PREP TIME
26 HRS

COOK TIME
4–5 HRS

SERVES
2

HEAT
INDIRECT
225°F (107°C)

COOKING SURFACE
STANDARD GRATE

Smoky and tender, these ribs have a flavorful exterior thanks to the beer-based brine, and they're delicious with or without BBQ sauce. If you're cooking for a crowd, you can easily scale up.

BEER-INFUSED BABY BACK RIBS

INGREDIENTS

1 rack of baby back ribs, about 3lb (1.4kg) in total
BBQ sauce, to serve

for the brine

¾ cup kosher salt
⅓ cup packed light brown sugar
⅓ cup raw sugar
1½ tsp pink curing salt
3 cups hot water
2 cups beer, preferably brown ale or lager
2 tbsp pickling spice

to smoke

apple or apricot wood chunks

METHOD

1 To make the brine, in a large bowl, whisk together kosher salt, brown sugar, raw sugar, pink curing salt, and hot water until sugars and salts dissolve. Whisk in beer and pickling spice, and set aside to cool to room temperature.

2 Place ribs on a cutting board and remove the thin, papery membrane from the back of the ribs. Cut the rack in half widthwise between the middle bones. Place ribs in a heavy-duty resealable plastic bag and add brine to cover. Squeeze out any excess air and place in an aluminum pan or a roasting pan. (Any extra brine can be refrigerated and saved for a later use.) Refrigerate for 24 hours.

3 Remove ribs from the brine and pat dry with paper towels. Arrange ribs on a wire rack over a rimmed baking sheet and let dry uncovered in the fridge for 2 hours.

4 Preheat the grill to 225°F (107°C). Once hot, add the wood chunks and install the heat deflector and a standard grate. Place ribs bone side down on the grate, close the lid, and smoke until the meat shrinks back from the ends of the bones by ½ inch (1.25cm), about 4 to 5 hours. Transfer ribs to a cutting board and cut into individual ribs.

5 Place ribs on a serving platter, brush with BBQ sauce, and serve immediately. (For more charring and caramelization, return the sauce-coated ribs to the grill for 5 to 10 minutes more before serving.)

TIP
Curing salts are used for food preservation, not seasoning, and contain sodium nitrite. Use a pink curing salt, such as Insta Cure, for this recipe.

PREP TIME
8-16 HRS

COOK TIME
3-4 HRS

SERVES
6

HEAT
**INDIRECT
300°F (149°C)**

COOKING SURFACE
MULTI-TIERED RACK

A cayenne-spiked rub gives these ribs a spicy flavor and crisp bark—the chewy, jerky-like crust that forms on smoked meats. For more tender bark, wrap in foil for the last two hours of smoking.

SPICY BBQ SPARE RIBS

INGREDIENTS

6lb (2.7kg) spare ribs, trimmed and membrane removed

for the marinade
1 cup cider vinegar
1 cup apple cider
4 garlic cloves, minced
2 bay leaves
2 tbsp hot sauce
1 tbsp kosher salt

for the sauce
¾ cup apple cider vinegar
¾ cups apple cider
1 tbsp hot sauce

for the rub
½ cup packed light brown sugar
3 tbsp chili powder
1 tbsp smoked paprika
2 tbsp granulated garlic
2 tbsp onion powder
1 tsp ground cayenne pepper
1 tbsp kosher salt
2 tsp ground cumin
½ tsp ground cinnamon
1 tsp ground black pepper

to smoke
pecan wood chunks

METHOD

1 To make the marinade, in a shallow nonreactive pan large enough to hold ribs, combine vinegar, cider, garlic, bay leaves, hot sauce, and salt. Place ribs in the marinade, turn to coat, and cover with plastic wrap. Refrigerate for 8 hours or up to 16 hours, turning once. Before grilling, remove ribs from the marinade and allow to come to room temperature.

2 To make the rub, in a medium bowl, combine all the rub ingredients. Sprinkle the ribs all over with ½ cup rub, patting it on with your fingers. Wrap tightly with plastic wrap and refrigerate for 90 minutes.

3 Preheat the grill to 300°F (149°C). Once hot, add the wood chunks and install the heat deflector and a multi-tiered rack.

4 To make the sauce, in a medium bowl, whisk together vinegar, cider, and hot sauce. Place ribs flat on the rack, close the lid, and smoke until the edges are crispy and the meat has pulled back from the bone, about 3 to 4 hours. Brush with the sauce every hour, and turn once during grilling.

5 Remove ribs from the grill, brush with any remaining sauce, and serve immediately.

 TIP To trim the ribs, place meat side up on a cutting board. Cut along the line of fat at the base to remove the cartilaginous rib tips. Flip, cut off the flap of meat on the inside, and remove the membrane.

Freshly smoked bacon is unlike anything you'll find at the supermarket. Smoking pulls the flavors of the wood as well as the curing spices into the meat, giving the bacon a deep red color.

FRESH SMOKED BACON

INGREDIENTS

1 skinned pork belly, about 4–5lb (1.8–2.3kg) in total

for the cure

⅓ cup kosher salt

3 tbsp ground black pepper

2 tsp pink curing salt

⅓ cup packed light brown sugar, granulated sugar, or maple sugar or a mixture of all three

to smoke

hickory, oak, mesquite, or any fruit wood chunks

METHOD

1 To make the cure, in a large bowl, combine kosher salt, pepper, curing salt, and sugar. Rub the cure on both sides of pork belly. Place pork in an airtight container and cure for 5 days in the fridge, turning pork over each day.

2 Rinse pork and pat dry with paper towels. Refrigerate uncovered for at least 3 hours or overnight, turning once or twice.

3 Preheat the grill to 225°F (107°C). Once hot, add the wood chunks and install the heat deflector and standard grate. Place pork on the grate, close the lid, and smoke until the internal temperature reaches 165°F (74°C), about 2 to 3 hours.

4 Remove pork from the grill and cool as quickly as possible. (Use two pans with ice cubes between them, placing pork in the top pan.) Wrap tightly in plastic wrap and refrigerate overnight. Bacon can then be sliced and used as needed.

5 To cook the sliced bacon on the grate, preheat the grill to 375°F (191°C) using indirect heat with a cast iron grate or a cast iron griddle installed. Place bacon on the grate, close the lid, and grill until bacon reaches your desired texture, about 20 to 25 minutes.

 When slicing your bacon, consider how you plan on using it. Thinly sliced bacon cooks more quickly and more evenly, making it ideal for wrapping around other meats.

PREP TIME
3-5 HRS

COOK TIME
35 MINS

SERVES
6-8

HEAT
DIRECT
350°F (177°C)

COOKING SURFACE
CAST IRON GRATE

Pork loin is brined and brushed with a citrusy, sweet-and-spicy glaze. Serve thinly sliced on grilled baguette rounds for an elegant starter or pair with a crisp green salad as a main dish.

CITRUS PORK LOIN
with chipotle & honey glaze

INGREDIENTS

1½lb (680g) boneless pork loin roast, trimmed

kosher salt and freshly ground black pepper

1 baguette, sliced

for the brine

⅔ cup kosher salt

⅔ cup packed light brown sugar

4 tbsp pickling spice

8 cups hot water

½ cup orange juice

for the glaze

½ cup orange juice

¾ cup honey

3 tbsp puréed chipotle peppers in adobo sauce

1 tbsp Dijon mustard

3 tbsp ancho chili powder

3 tbsp canola oil

1½ tsp ground coriander

1½ tsp ground cumin

1½ tsp Spanish paprika

METHOD

1 To make the brine, in a large bowl, whisk together salt, brown sugar, pickling spice, and water until salt and sugar have dissolved. Add ice cubes a few at a time until the liquid is no longer hot. Place pork in a large resealable bag, and add ½ cup orange juice and enough brine to cover. (Any extra brine can be refrigerated and saved for later use.) Squeeze out any excess air and refrigerate for 3 to 5 hours.

2 To make the glaze, in a medium saucepan, combine all the glaze ingredients. Place on the stovetop over medium heat and simmer until thick, about 10 minutes, stirring occasionally. Season with salt and pepper to taste, and set aside to cool to room temperature.

3 Preheat the grill to 350°F (177°C) using direct heat with a cast iron grate installed. Remove pork from the brine, pat dry with paper towels, and allow to come to room temperature. Season with salt and pepper to taste, then place pork on the grate, positioning it near the edge to keep the glaze from burning. Close the lid and grill until the internal temperature reaches 140°F (60°C), about15 minutes per pound (approximately 30 minutes per kilogram). Turn the meat every 3 minutes while cooking, brushing with the glaze each time.

4 Transfer pork to a serving platter and brush with more glaze. Let rest for several minutes. While pork rests, place the baguette slices on the grate and toast for 1 to 2 minutes per side. Thinly slice pork and serve with the grilled baguette slices.

PREP TIME
2-4 HRS

COOK TIME
30-45 MINS

SERVES
6

HEAT
**INDIRECT
400°F (204°C)**

COOKING SURFACE
STANDARD GRATE

This is a dish for autumn, when apples are ripe and the days are cool. Scotch whisky flavors the brine and the brown sugar glaze, and grilled apples provide a sweet counterpart to the juicy meat.

WHISKY-GLAZED PORK TENDERLOIN

INGREDIENTS

2 pork tenderloins, about 3lb (1.4kg) in total, trimmed and silverskin removed

2 Granny Smith apples, cored and halved

for the brine

¼ cup kosher salt

¼ cup packed light brown sugar

2 tbsp pickling spice

½ cup Scotch whisky

¼ cup grated fresh horseradish (or use jarred)

3 cups hot water

for the glaze

½ tsp cinnamon

2 tbsp light brown sugar

2 tbsp raw sugar

¼ cup agave nectar

½ tsp ground cayenne

2 tbsp Scotch whisky

METHOD

1 To make the brine, in a medium bowl, whisk together salt, brown sugar, pickling spice, whisky, horseradish, and water until salt and sugar have dissolved. Place pork in a resealable plastic bag and add brine to cover. (Any extra brine can be refrigerated and saved for a later use.) Refrigerate for 2 to 4 hours.

2 To make the glaze, in a small bowl, whisk together cinnamon, brown sugar, raw sugar, agave nectar, cayenne, and whisky. Reserve half the glaze and set aside. Remove pork from the brine, pat dry with paper towels, and brush with the remaining glaze. Let sit at room temperature for 30 minutes before roasting.

3 Preheat the grill to 400°F (204°C) using indirect heat with a drip pan on the heat deflector and a standard grate installed. Place glazed pork on the grate, close the lid, and roast until pork reaches an internal temperature of 140°F (60°C), about 20 to 30 minutes. Brush pork with more glaze halfway through the cooking process.

4 Brush apples on all sides with the reserved glaze. Place cut side up on the grate around pork and grill until beginning to soften and the glaze begins to thickens, about 10 to 15 minutes, brushing with more glaze while cooking.

5 Remove pork and apples from the grill and let rest for 5 to 10 minutes. Slice pork and apples before serving.

PREP TIME
30 MINS

COOK TIME
4½ HRS

SERVES
8

HEAT
**INDIRECT
300°F (149°C)**

COOKING SURFACE
**STANDARD GRATE
DUTCH OVEN**

Pork belly is braised and then roasted, resulting in deliciously tender meat with a crisp exterior that's complemented by the creamy grits. Kimchi and pickled vegetables add tangy spice.

PORK BELLY & RICE GRITS

INGREDIENTS

3 tbsp vegetable oil

2lb pork belly, about 1 in (2.5-cm) thick, cut into 8 pieces

kosher salt and freshly ground black pepper

1 small red onion, roughly chopped

2 small carrots, roughly chopped

1 bay leaf

½ tsp coriander seeds

4 cups chicken stock, divided

¼ cup rice flour

½ cup rice grits or hominy grits

½ cup heavy cream

1 cup shredded sharp Cheddar cheese or Fontina (optional)

½ cup finely chopped kimchi

for the pickles

½ tsp sugar

¼ cup unseasoned rice vinegar

½ cup thinly sliced radishes

½ red onion

2 scallions, thinly sliced on the bias

to smoke

oak, apricot, or bourbon barrel wood chunks

METHOD

1 Preheat the grill to 300°F (149°C). Once hot, add the wood chunks and install the heat deflector along with a standard grate and Dutch oven. To the hot Dutch oven, heat oil until shimmering. Add pork pieces, and season with salt and pepper to taste. Close the grill lid and smoke until pork has browned on all sides, about 10 to 15 minutes. Add onion, carrots, bay leaf, and coriander seeds, close the grill lid, and cook for 5 minutes more.

2 Add 2 cups chicken stock, close the grill lid, and cook until the meat is very tender, about 3 hours. Leave the lid off the Dutch oven for the first hour and cover for the remaining cooking time. Transfer cooked pork to a cutting board and let cool slightly. Cut each piece in half crosswise, lightly coat with rice flour, and set aside. Discard the vegetables and reserve the braising liquid.

3 Rinse the Dutch oven and return it to the grill. Open the top and bottom vents to raise the grill temperature to 350°F (177°C). Once hot, arrange the floured pork pieces on the grate around the Dutch oven (not inside). Roast until the fat has rendered and pork is slightly crispy, about 15 to 20 minutes.

4 Place grits in the Dutch oven and toast until just shiny, about 3 minutes. Slowly add cream and the remaining 2 cups stock in three different stages and cook until creamy and tender, about 10 to 15 minutes, stirring every 3 minutes to break up any lumps. Add cheese (if using), and season with salt and pepper to taste.

5 To make the pickles, in a large shallow bowl, whisk together sugar and vinegar until sugar dissolves. Add onions, scallions, and radishes, cover with plastic wrap, and refrigerate for 15 minutes.

6 On the stovetop in a medium saucepan, bring the reserved braising liquid to a boil. Simmer until the volume has decreased by half, about 15 to 20 minutes.

7 Transfer pork and grits to serving dishes. Stir the reduced braising liquid into the grits or as much for the desired consistency, and season with salt and pepper to taste. Serve immediately with kimchi and pickled onions, scallions, and radishes.

PREP TIME
25 MINS

COOK TIME
20 MINS

SERVES
6

HEAT
DIRECT
425°F (218°C)

COOKING SURFACE
STANDARD GRATE
CAST IRON SKILLET

This salty, savory noodle dish elevates the familiar flavors of Chinese takeout with tender stir-fried pork and fresh vegetables. Lo mein egg noodles, udon noodles, or soba noodles all work well.

HOISIN PORK & NOODLES

INGREDIENTS

8oz (225g) lo mein egg noodles

¼lb (115g) pork tenderloin, trimmed and silverskin removed

½ cup hoisin sauce, plus more for coating pork

2 tsp toasted sesame oil, divided

4 garlic cloves, minced

2 tsp grated fresh ginger

1 red or yellow bell pepper, cut into thin strips

2oz (55g) snow peas, cut into bite-sized pieces

½ cup low-sodium chicken stock

1 tbsp cornstarch

1 tbsp low-sodium soy sauce

4 scallions, thinly sliced, to garnish

¼ cup chopped cashews, to garnish

METHOD

1 Preheat the grill to 425°F (218°C) using direct heat with a standard grate installed and a cast iron skillet on the grate. While the grill heats, cook the noodles on the stovetop according to package directions. Drain and rinse under cold water, then drain again and set aside.

2 Cut pork crosswise into ¼-in (.5-cm) slices, then cut the slices in half. Brush pork lightly with a little hoisin sauce. In the hot skillet, heat 1 tsp oil until shimmering. Add pork, garlic, and ginger, and stir-fry until pork is no longer pink, about 3 minutes. Transfer pork to a bowl.

3 Return the skillet to the grill, add the bell pepper and snow peas, and stir-fry for 1 minute. While pepper and peas cook, in a small bowl, whisk together stock and cornstarch. Add the stock mixture, hoisin sauce, and soy sauce to the skillet. Bring to a boil, stirring constantly, then add pork back to the skillet. Stir-fry until pork is cooked through, about 1 minute. Add noodles and the remaining 1 tsp sesame oil to the mixture and stir.

4 Transfer everything to a large serving bowl, sprinkle sliced scallions and chopped cashews over top, and serve immediately.

PREP TIME
25 MINS

COOK TIME
25–40 MINS

SERVES
6

HEAT
**INDIRECT
300°F (149°C)**

COOKING SURFACE
**STANDARD GRATE
DUTCH OVEN**

Perfect for cool evenings, this rustic soup is flavored with garlic, onion, and paprika and loaded with chunks of pork and hearty white beans. Serve with crusty bread to sop up the savory broth.

PORK, WHITE BEAN & KALE SOUP

INGREDIENTS

1 tbsp extra virgin olive oil

1lb (450g) pork tenderloin, trimmed and cut into 1-in (2.5-cm) pieces

¾ tsp kosher salt

1 medium yellow onion, finely diced

4 garlic cloves, minced

2 tsp smoked paprika

¼ tsp crushed red pepper flakes (optional)

1 cup dry white wine

4 Roma tomatoes, chopped

4 cups low-sodium chicken stock

1 bunch of kale, ribs removed and leaves chopped

15oz (425g) can white beans, drained and rinsed

crusty French bread, to serve

METHOD

1 Preheat the grill to 300°F (149°C) using indirect heat with a Dutch oven on the heat deflector. In the hot Dutch oven, heat oil until shimmering. Add pork pieces and sprinkle with salt. Close the grill lid and cook until pork is no longer pink on the outside, about 2 minutes, stirring once or twice. Transfer pork to a bowl, leaving the juices in the Dutch oven.

2 Return the Dutch oven to the grill and add the onion. Close the grill lid and cook until beginning to brown, about 2 to 3 minutes, stirring a few times. Add garlic, paprika, and red pepper flakes (if using), close the grill lid, and cook until fragrant, about 30 seconds, stirring once or twice. Add wine and tomatoes, and stir to scrape up any browned bits. Add stock, close the lid, and heat until beginning to simmer, about 5 to 10 minutes.

3 Once simmering, add kale and stir until wilted, about 5 to 8 minutes. Close the top and bottom vents to reduce the heat, and simmer until kale is tender, about 5 to 8 minutes more, stirring occasionally. Stir in beans, reserved pork, and any accumulated juices. Simmer until beans are heated and pork is fully cooked, about 2 to 5 minutes. Remove the Dutch oven from the grill, and serve immediately with crusty bread.

TIP For a smoky version of this soup, add one or two small chunks of smoking wood to the coals before installing the heat deflector. Choose apple, grapevine, bourbon, or wine barrels.

PREP TIME	COOK TIME	SERVES	HEAT	COOKING SURFACE
2-24 HRS	**15-20 MINS**	**6**	**DIRECT** **425ºF (218ºC)**	**CAST IRON GRATE** **DUTCH OVEN**

Fruity and spicy, this brightly colored curry is flavored with fragrant cumin, cinnamon, cardamom, and ginger. Sweet but tart mango pickles complement the tender pieces of marinated pork.

PORK CURRY
with pickled mango & rice

INGREDIENTS

2 pork tenderloins, about 3lb (1.4kg) in total, trimmed, silverskin removed, and cut into 2-in (.5-cm) pieces

3 cups cooked white rice

naan bread, to serve (optional)

for the marinade

4 dried red chile peppers

⅓ cup white vinegar

2 tsp ground cumin

1 tsp ground black pepper

½ tsp cinnamon

3 tsp ground cardamom

1 tsp ground cloves

pinch of ground nutmeg

1 tsp grated fresh ginger

5 garlic cloves, peeled

½ cup olive oil

2 medium yellow onions, roughly chopped

1 tsp sugar

kosher salt

for the pickled mango

½ cup apple cider vinegar

1 tbsp sugar

½ tsp kosher salt

1 cup hot water

1 tbsp Vindaloo curry seasoning

1 ripe mango, peeled and sliced

METHOD

1 To make the marinade, in a small bowl, cover peppers with vinegar and let soak for 10 minutes. Transfer peppers and vinegar to a food processor, add remaining marinade ingredients, and blend until smooth. Transfer half the marinade to a resealable plastic bag. Reserve the remaining marinade and set aside.

2 Place pork pieces in the bag with the marinade and squeeze out any excess air. Refrigerate for at least 2 hours and up to 24 hours. Before grilling, remove from the fridge and bring to room temperature.

3 To make the pickled mango, in a small bowl, whisk together vinegar, sugar, and salt until sugar and salt have dissolved. Pack mango in a small jar and pour the vinegar mixture over top to cover. Let sit at room temperature for 1 hour.

4 Preheat the grill to 425°F (218°C) using direct heat with a cast iron grate installed and a Dutch oven on the grate. Remove pork pieces from the marinade and place on the grate around the Dutch oven (not inside). Close the grill lid and grill until the internal temperature reaches 140°F (60°C), about 8 to 12 minutes.

5 Transfer the grilled pork pieces to the Dutch oven and add the cooked rice, reserved marinade, and pickled mango. (Discard pickling liquid or refrigerate in a sealable container for future use.) Cook until warmed through, about 5 to 7 minutes, stir occasionally. Serve immediately with warm naan (if desired).

 TIP You can make the pickled mango up to 2 weeks ahead of time. Prepare as directed, cover, and refrigerate until needed. You can also double the ingredients and use the pickled mango for other recipes.

PREP TIME
4-24 HRS

COOK TIME
20-30 MINS

SERVES
4-8

HEAT
DIRECT
425°F (218°C)

COOKING SURFACE
CAST IRON GRATE
CAST IRON SKILLET

Marinated pork and grilled vegetables simmer in an Asian-inspired sauce to create an aromatic filling for crisp lettuce leaves. Serve as a starter or on their own for a light meal.

PORK LETTUCE WRAPS

INGREDIENTS

¼ head of napa cabbage

2 carrots, peeled

½ head of broccoli, trimmed and cut into large pieces

1½lb (680g) pork tenderloin, diced into small cubes

2 tbsp canola oil

½ cup water chestnuts, drained and thinly sliced

1 head of Bibb or iceberg lettuce, separated into leaves, to serve

1 bunch of scallions, sliced

for the marinade

¼ cup chopped fresh basil leaves

¼ cup chopped fresh mint leaves

¼ cup chopped fresh cilantro

¼ cup thinly sliced fresh ginger

2 tbsp chopped garlic

½ cup canola oil

½ lime, cut into 8 pieces

2 tbsp kosher salt

for the sauce

¼ cup white wine

¼ cup low-sodium soy sauce

2 tbsp hoisin sauce

1 tbsp rice wine vinegar

1 tbsp sugar

1 tbsp cornstarch

1½ tsp chili garlic sauce

METHOD

1 To make the marinade, in a large bowl, combine all the marinade ingredients. Add pork to the marinade, and stir to coat. Cover with plastic wrap and refrigerate for at least 4 hours or overnight.

2 To make the sauce, in a small bowl, combine all the sauce ingredients. Set aside.

3 Preheat the grill to 425°F (218°C) using direct heat with a cast iron grate installed and a cast iron skillet on the grate. Arrange cabbage, carrots, and broccoli on the grate around the skillet. Close the lid and grill until beginning to soften and char, about 7 to 10 minutes. Remove the vegetables from the grill. Once cool enough to handle, finely shred the cabbage, julienne the carrots, and cut the broccoli into small pieces. Set aside.

4 Add oil to the skillet and heat until shimmering. Remove pork from the marinade and add to the skillet, discarding the marinade. Close the lid and grill until the meat is seared on all sides, about 3 to 5 minutes, stirring occasionally.

5 Add cabbage, carrots, broccoli, and water chestnuts to the skillet, close the lid, and cook for 2 to 3 minutes. Stir in the sauce, close the lid, and cook until the sauce has thickened, about 8 to 10 minutes.

6 Remove the skillet from the grill. To serve, scoop some of the pork and vegetable mixture into each lettuce leaf and top with scallions.

PREP TIME **55 MINS**	COOK TIME **30 MINS**	SERVES **8**	HEAT **INDIRECT** **475°F (246°C)**	COOKING SURFACE **STANDARD GRATE**

Savory and satisfying, these sausage-wrapped eggs are quintessential British picnic fare. In this version, crispy bacon replaces the traditional breaded exterior for extra meaty flavor.

BACON-WRAPPED SCOTCH EGGS
with mayonnaise & mustard sauce

INGREDIENTS

8 large eggs

1lb (450g) pork sausage, casings removed

16 bacon strips

for the sauce

1 cup mayonnaise

1 cup coarse ground mustard

kosher salt and freshly ground black pepper

METHOD

1 On the stovetop over high heat, bring a large pot of water to a boil. Once boiling, add eggs and boil for 4 minutes. Carefully drain, then transfer eggs to an ice bath to chill for 30 minutes. Peel and set aside.

2 To make the sauce, in a small bowl, combine mayonnaise and mustard, and season with salt and pepper to taste. Refrigerate until ready to serve.

3 Preheat the grill to 475°F (246°C) using indirect heat with a standard grate installed. Divide the sausage into 8 equal portions. Form one portion of sausage meat into a thin, flat patty and gently wrap it around one egg, making sure the egg is fully enclosed in an even layer of meat. Repeat with the remaining sausage and eggs, then wrap each egg with 2 bacon strips, completely covering the sausage with bacon.

4 Place eggs directly on the grate, close the lid, and cook until the sausage is cooked through and the bacon is crisp, about 20 minutes. Rotate the eggs a few times while cooking to ensure the bacon gets crispy.

5 Remove eggs from the grill, cut them in half, and arrange on a serving dish. Serve immediately with the sauce.

TIP — Choose a high-quality pork sausage with seasonings that appeal to your palate. Breakfast sausage or spicy Italian sausage are good choices.

PREP TIME
25 DAYS

COOK TIME
30-40 MINS

SERVES
12

HEAT
**INDIRECT
200°F (93°C)**

COOKING SURFACE
STANDARD GRATE

This is a homemade version of lomo embuchado, the Spanish cured tenderloin often served as a tapa. It takes time to make but is delicious in sandwiches, paired with eggs, or on pizza or crackers.

CURED PORK TENDERLOIN

INGREDIENTS

2 pork tenderloins, about 3lb (1.4kg) in total, trimmed and silverskin removed

for the cure

3 tbsp kosher salt

1 tbsp sugar

1 tsp pink curing salt

2 tsp ground black pepper

1 tsp garlic powder

1 tsp ground cloves

2 tsp onion powder

1½ tsp dried thyme

smoked paprika, to coat

to smoke

apple wood chunks

METHOD

1 To make the cure, in a small bowl, combine all the cure ingredients. Rub the mixture into pork, apply a coat of paprika on top of the rub, wrap tightly with plastic wrap, and refrigerate for 12 days.

2 After 12 days of curing, remove pork from the plastic, rinse it off, and let dry on a cooling rack in the fridge for 2 to 3 hours. It should be red in color and dry on the surface.

3 Preheat the grill to 200°F (93°C). Once hot, add the wood chunks and install the heat deflector and a standard grate. Truss the meat with kitchen twine as you would a roast, leaving a long loop at one end to hang the meat. (You can also use premade sausage netting.) Close the lid and smoke until meat reaches an internal temperature of 120°F (49°C), about 30 to 40 minutes. (Pork should still look somewhat red in color after smoking.) After smoking, hang the meat in a cool, humid place (70 percent humidity is ideal) to dry for 12 days.

4 After drying for 12 days, the meat should feel firm throughout and be a pleasing red color. It's now ready to slice and serve. To store the cured pork, wrap tightly in butcher paper and refrigerate. Pork will last for several months in the fridge if untouched, but once it's been sliced, it will last a week or two.

 TIP White mold is your friend, green mold isn't good, and black mold is dangerous. At the first sight of green or black mold, wipe down the meat with a cloth wetted with vinegar.

PREP TIME
4–6 HRS

COOK TIME
16–20 MINS

SERVES
12

HEAT
DIRECT
400ºF (204ºC)

COOKING SURFACE
CAST IRON GRATE

Creamy slaw and tender pork medallions are all you need to fill your slider buns with a savory meal that's equal parts crunchy and crispy. A bourbon-infused glaze provides an extra highlight.

PORK TENDERLOIN SLIDERS
with fennel, apple & mustard slaw

INGREDIENTS

3lb (1.4kg) pork tenderloin
kosher salt and freshly ground
  black pepper
12 slider buns or rolls

for the brine
½ cup kosher salt
½ cup packed light brown sugar
3 tbsp pickling spice
6 cups hot water

for the glaze
12oz (340g) apple juice
1 cup bourbon
3 tbsp dark brown sugar
1 tbsp Dijon mustard
½ tsp kosher salt
½ tsp crushed red pepper flakes

for the slaw
2 tbsp mayonnaise
2 tbsp whole grain mustard
juice of 1 lemon
2 tbsp plain Greek yogurt
3 tbsp chopped fresh dill
1 fennel bulb, julienned
2 Granny Smith apples, julienned
1 red onion, thinly sliced into
  half-moons

METHOD

1 To make the brine, in a medium bowl, whisk together salt, brown sugar, pickling spice, and hot water until salt and sugar have dissolved. Add ice cubes a few at a time until the liquid is no longer hot. Pour the brine into a large resealable plastic bag, place pork tenderloin in the bag, and refrigerate for 2 to 4 hours. (Any extra brine can be refrigerated and saved for a later use.)

2 To make the slaw, in a large bowl, combine mayonnaise, mustard, lemon juice, Greek yogurt, and dill. Add fennel, apples, and onion. Season with salt and pepper to taste. Stir to combine, cover with plastic wrap, and refrigerate for 2 hours.

3 To make the glaze, in a medium saucepan, combine apple juice, bourbon, sugar, mustard, and salt. Bring to a boil on the stovetop over medium-high heat, then reduce heat to medium and simmer until the mixture has reduced to 1 cup, about 10 minutes, stirring occasionally. Stir in red pepper flakes, remove the saucepan from the heat, and refrigerate until needed.

4 Remove pork from the brine, pat dry with paper towels, place on a cutting board, and slice into medallions. Allow pork to come to room temperature, and season with salt and pepper to taste.

5 Preheat the grill to 400°F (204°C) using direct heat and a cast iron grate installed. Brush medallions on both sides with the glaze, place pork on grate, and close the lid. Cook for 3 to 5 minutes per side, brushing with glaze once or twice. Remove pork from the grill and serve topped with slaw on toasted slider buns.

PREP TIME
2–24 HRS

COOK TIME
4½ HRS

SERVES
8

HEAT
**INDIRECT
275°F (135°C)**

COOKING SURFACE
STANDARD GRATE

In this version of the traditional spit-roasted dish, thin slices of pork are coated in sauce, then stacked and smoked, allowing the fat to render and permeate the meat with succulent flavor.

TACOS AL PASTOR

INGREDIENTS

4lb (1.8kg) pork roast, thinly sliced at the butcher

1 small pineapple, peeled, cored, and cut lengthwise into quarters

for the sauce

4 tsp vegetable oil

4 tbsp ancho chile powder

4 tbsp pasilla chile powder

2 tsp Mexican oregano

2 tsp ground cumin

2 tbsp achiote powder or paste

½ cup white vinegar

5 tsp kosher salt

4 tsp sugar

2 chipotle peppers in adobo

6 garlic cloves, peeled

to serve

32 x 6-in (15.25-cm) corn tortillas, heated and kept warm

1 medium white onion, finely diced

1 bunch of fresh cilantro, roughly chopped

1 cup jarred salsa

3 limes, cut into wedges

to smoke

peach, apple, or pecan wood chunks

METHOD

1 Preheat the grill to 275°F (135°C). Once hot, add the wood chunks and install the heat deflector and a standard grate.

2 To make the sauce, on the stovetop in a saucepan over medium-high heat, heat oil until shimmering. Add ancho chile powder, pasilla chile powder, oregano, cumin, and achiote powder, and cook for 2 minutes. Add vinegar, salt, sugar, and chipotle peppers, and cook for 30 more seconds. Transfer the mixture to a blender and add the garlic. Blend on high speed until completely smooth, about 1 minute. Transfer sauce to a large bowl.

3 Add pork to the sauce, and toss until each piece is well coated. In a disposable aluminum baking dish, pile pork slices in a single layer, forming a tower. (The pork tower will extend beyond the rim of the pan.) Place the pan on the grate, close the lid, and cook until the meat is cooked through and completely tender, about 4 hours. (Pork will drip a lot.) Remove the pan from the grill and allow to cool slightly. Cover with aluminum foil and refrigerate for at least 2 hours or overnight.

4 Preheat the grill to 350°F (177°C) using indirect heat with a standard grate installed and a cast iron skillet on the grate. Remove pork from the fridge and scrape off the solidified fat. Slice vertically through the pork tower, creating fine shavings of meat.

5 Add the shaved pork to the hot skillet along with the pineapple quarters. Close the grill lid and cook until the meat is hot and tender and pineapple begins to soften, about 30 minutes, stirring occasionally.

6 Remove pork and pineapple from the grill. Serve wrapped in double-stacked corn tortillas and topped with onion, cilantro, salsa, and a squeeze of lime.

PREP TIME
10 MINS

COOK TIME
3½ HRS

SERVES
16

HEAT
**INDIRECT
300°F (149°C)**

COOKING SURFACE
**STANDARD GRATE
ROASTING PAN**

This recipe elevates the traditional supermarket smoked ham with a second smoking on the kamado and a sweet-and-spicy glaze. The resulting meat is deeply flavored with a caramelized exterior.

TWICE-SMOKED HAM
with cinnamon & bourbon glaze

INGREDIENTS

18lb (8kg) bone-in whole or spiral-cut smoked ham, at room temperature

1 cup water

for the glaze

1 cup sugar

2 tbsp water

1 tbsp fennel seeds

1 tbsp coriander seeds

4 star anise pods

4 bay leaves

2 cinnamon sticks

2 garlic cloves

1-in (2.5-cm) piece fresh ginger, thinly sliced

1 dried red chile pepper

1 tsp finely grated orange zest

2 cups bourbon

2 tbsp low-sodium soy sauce

2 tbsp honey

to smoke

hickory or apple wood chunks

METHOD

1 Preheat the grill to 300°F (149°C) using indirect heat. Once hot, add the wood chunks and install the heat deflector and a standard grate. Place the precooked ham in a large roasting pan (a disposable aluminum pan works well) and add water. Place the pan on the grate, close the lid, and smoke until an instant-read thermometer inserted in the thickest part of the meat reads 120°F (49°C), about 2 hours and 45 minutes, basting occasionally with any accumulated juices.

2 To make the glaze, in a medium saucepan, combine sugar and water, and place the pan on the stovetop over medium-high heat. Cook until a light golden syrup forms, about 8 to 10 minutes, swirling the pan occasionally.

3 Remove from the heat and quickly add fennel seeds, coriander seeds, star anise, bay leaves, cinnamon, garlic, ginger, chile pepper, and orange zest. Let sit until fragrant, about 20 seconds. Carefully add the bourbon, soy sauce, and honey. Return the glaze to medium heat and bring to a simmer until slightly thickened, about 10 minutes, stirring occasionally.

4 Once ham reaches 120°F (49°C), brush it with the glaze. Continue smoking until the top is lightly caramelized, about 30 minutes more, brushing with glaze every 10 minutes.

5 Transfer ham to a platter and let rest for 15 minutes. Skim the fat from the pan and transfer the juices to a bowl. Slice and serve with the warm pan juices.

PREP TIME
2 HRS

COOK TIME
4 HRS

SERVES
12

HEAT
**INDIRECT
350°F (177°C)**

COOKING SURFACE
STANDARD GRATE

A twist on the quintessential Guadalajara dish, these hearty sandwiches feature thinly sliced smoked pork piled on a soft submarine bun and soaked in a spicy, tomato-based sauce.

PORK TORTAS AHOGADA

INGREDIENTS

16 garlic cloves, minced

2 tbsp fresh oregano, minced

¼ cup kosher salt, plus more as needed

¼ ground black pepper, plus more as needed

9lb (4.1kg) boneless pork butt

12 hoagie buns

for the sauce

6 tbsp vegetable oil

4 medium white onions, chopped

8 garlic cloves, minced

4 x 28oz (794g) cans whole peeled tomatoes

8 chipotle peppers in adobo

5 tsp dried oregano

1½ tsp kosher salt

¼ tsp sugar

to smoke

grapevine, peach, or oak wood chunks

METHOD

1 In a small bowl, combine garlic, oregano, salt, and pepper. Use a sharp knife to make 1-in (2.5-cm) cuts all over pork. Fill the cuts with the garlic mixture, and rub the exterior of the meat with more salt and pepper to taste.

2 Preheat the grill to 350°F (177°C). Once hot, add the wood chunks and install the heat deflector and a standard grate. Place pork in a shallow roasting pan (a disposable aluminum pan works well) and place the pan on the grate. Close the lid and roast until pork is tender, cooked through, and reaches an internal temperature of 190°F (88°C), about 2 to 3 hours. Remove pork from the grill and let rest for 20 minutes before slicing thinly, reserving the pan drippings.

3 To make the sauce, in a large pot on the stovetop over high heat, heat oil until almost smoking. Add onion and garlic, lower the heat to medium-high, and sauté until onion is translucent, about 2 to 3 minutes. Add the reserved pan drippings, tomatoes, peppers, oregano, salt, and sugar, and lower the heat to a simmer. Cook uncovered until the sauce is hot and the vegetables begin to soften, about 10 to 15 minutes, stirring frequently. Using an immersion blender, purée the sauce, then strain through a mesh sieve, using a spoon to press the liquid through.

4 Slice rolls in half lengthwise, removing some of the insides. Spoon 2 tbsp chipotle sauce over each half, top with the sliced pork, then spoon ¼ cup sauce over each torta. Place tortas in a clean roasting pan and return to the grill until heated through, about 2 to 3 minutes. Serve immediately with any remaining sauce.

TIP Bulk up your sandwich with sliced avocado, sliced habanero peppers, and sour cream mixed with chopped onion, garlic, and cilantro. Or add your own favorite toppings.

PREP TIME **25 MINS**	COOK TIME **3 HRS**	SERVES **12**	HEAT **DIRECT** **325ºF (163ºC)**	COOKING SURFACE **CAST IRON GRATE** **DUTCH OVEN**

Tender chunks of crawfish and smoky sausage are the stars of this hearty dish, which has a hint of heat from cayenne. Don't rush the roux—this is what gives the gumbo its rich, deep flavor.

SMOKED ANDOUILLE & CRAWFISH GUMBO

INGREDIENTS

1 green bell pepper, left whole
1 large yellow onion, halved
3 stalks of celery, left whole
1½ cups vegetable oil
½ cups all-purpose flour
½lb (225g) andouille sausage
1lb (450g) smoked sausage
8 cups chicken stock
1lb (450g) crawfish meat
1½ tsp kosher salt
½ tsp ground cayenne pepper (optional)
2 tbsp chopped fresh flat-leaf parsley
2 tbsp sliced scallions
6 cups cooked white rice, to serve (optional)

METHOD

1 Preheat the grill to 325°F (163°C) using direct heat with a cast iron grate installed and a Dutch oven on the grate. Place pepper, onion, and celery on the grate around the Dutch oven, close the grill lid, and grill until beginning to soften and char, about 6 to 8 minutes. Transfer the vegetables to a cutting board. Seed and dice the pepper, and dice the celery and onion. Set aside.

2 In the hot Dutch oven, heat oil until shimmering. Add flour and stir. Close the grill lid and cook for 20 to 25 minutes, stirring every 5 minutes. While the roux cooks, place the sausages on the grate next to the Dutch oven, close the grill lid, and grill until slightly charred, about 10 minutes. Remove the sausages from the grill, finely dice andouille and slice smoked sausage into bite-sized pieces.

3 Once the roux looks dark brown in color, add sausages, peppers, onions, and celery to the Dutch oven, and stir to coat. Close the grill lid and cook until the vegetables are soft, about 8 to 10 minutes.

4 Add stock to the Dutch oven, and stir until the roux and stock are well combined. Leaving the Dutch oven uncovered, close the grill lid and reduce the heat by closing the top and bottom vents most of the way. Cook for 90 minutes, stirring occasionally. Add crawfish to the Dutch oven, close the grill lid, and cook for 15 minutes more.

5 Remove the Dutch oven from the grill and let sit for 5 minutes before skimming any fat that has risen to the surface. Stir in salt and cayenne (if using). Taste and adjust the seasonings as needed. Stir in parsley and scallions, and serve immediately with white rice (if using).

POULTRY

PREP TIME
2–24 HRS

COOK TIME
45–65 MINS

SERVES
12

HEAT
DIRECT
425°F (218ºC)

COOKING SURFACE
CAST IRON GRATE

This crowd-friendly, Mexican-inspired dish is perfect for casual entertaining. The salad can be prepared several hours in advance, and the marinated chicken takes only a few minutes to grill.

GRILLED TEQUILA CHICKEN
with corn & black bean salad

INGREDIENTS

12 skinless, boneless chicken thighs, about 3lb (1.4kg) in total

for the marinade
juice of 4 limes
¼ cup olive oil
1 cup tequila
2 tsp kosher salt
5 garlic cloves
1 jalapeño pepper, sliced
½ bunch of fresh cilantro, chopped

for the salad
1 cup dried black beans
¼ cup tequila
2 cups vegetable stock
2 Roma tomatoes, diced
¼ cup diced orange bell pepper
¼ cup diced yellow onion
¼ cup diced scallions
¼ cup diced mango
1 tbsp chopped fresh cilantro
1 jalapeño pepper, seeded and minced
4 tbsp sherry vinegar
juice of 1 lime
3 tbsp honey
1 tbsp kosher salt
1 tsp ground black pepper
pinch of ground cumin
4 ears of corn, shucked

METHOD

1 To make the marinade, add all the marinade ingredients to a food processor and pulse until well combined. Place chicken thighs in a large resealable plastic bag and pour in the marinade mixture. Refrigerate for at least 2 hours or overnight.

2 Place black beans in a medium bowl and add tequila to cover. Cover with plastic wrap and refrigerate overnight. Drain beans and place in a saucepan on the stovetop. Add vegetable stock to cover by 1 inch (2.5cm) and bring to a boil. Reduce heat to a simmer, cover, and cook until beans are tender but not falling apart, about 30 to 45 minutes.

3 Drain beans and place in a large bowl. Add tomatoes, pepper, onion, scallions, mango, cilantro, jalapeño, vinegar, lime juice, honey, salt, pepper, and cumin. Stir gently until all ingredients are well mixed. Cover and refrigerate for at least 1 hour to allow the flavors to meld.

4 Preheat the grill to 425°F (218°C) using direct heat with a cast iron grate installed. Place corn on the grate and grill until lightly charred, about 6 to 8 minutes. Transfer the corn to a cutting board and cut the kernels from the cobs. Stir kernels into the black bean salad and set aside.

5 Remove chicken thighs from the marinade and place on the grate (discarding the marinade). Close the lid and grill until the internal temperature reaches 165°F (74°C), about 4 to 5 minutes per side, turning only once. Remove thighs from the grill, slice, and serve over the corn and black bean salad.

PREP TIME
8½ HRS

COOK TIME
15–25 MINS

SERVES
6

HEAT
DIRECT
375°F (191°C)

COOKING SURFACE
CAST IRON GRATE

A spicy coating of chili powder and rice flour is the secret to the crisp, flavorful skin of these addictive wings. The sweet-hot glaze adds another layer of irresistible flavor.

HONEY CHIPOTLE GRILLED WINGS

INGREDIENTS

3lb (1.4kg) chicken wings (about 18 wings), cut into sections

1 tbsp kosher salt

1 tbsp ground black pepper

1 tbsp chili powder

½ cup rice flour

1 tbsp chopped fresh cilantro, to garnish

for the brine

⅓ cup kosher salt

⅓ cup packed light brown sugar

2 tbsp pickling spice

4 cups hot water

for the glaze

3 chipotle peppers in adobo

1 tbsp adobo sauce

½ cup honey

2 tbsp fresh lemon juice

2 tbsp soy sauce

METHOD

1 To make the brine, in a medium bowl, whisk together salt, brown sugar, pickling spice, and water until salt and sugar have dissolved. Add ice cubes a few at a time until the liquid is no longer hot. Place chicken pieces into two resealable plastic bags and add brine to cover. (Any extra brine can be refrigerated and saved for a later use.) Refrigerate for 30 minutes.

2 In a large bowl, combine salt, pepper, chili powder, and rice flour. Working with a small amount of chicken at a time, dredge the meat, shaking off any excess flour. Arrange wings in a single layer on a wire rack placed over a baking pan. Refrigerate uncovered for 8 hours.

3 To make the glaze, combine peppers, honey, lemon juice, and soy sauce in a blender or food processor and purée until smooth. Transfer glaze to a small bowl.

4 Preheat the grill to 375°F (191°C) using direct heat with a cast iron grate installed. Remove chicken from the brine and pat dry with paper towels. Place wings skin side down on the grate, close the lid, and grill until the skin begins to brown and crisp, about 8 to 12 minutes per side. In the final 5 minutes of cooking, brush the glaze all over wings.

5 Transfer wings to a serving dish, coat with more glaze, sprinkle with cilantro, and serve immediately.

PREP TIME **2–24 HRS**	COOK TIME **40–55 MINS**	SERVES **6**	HEAT **INDIRECT 425°F (218°C)**	COOKING SURFACE **STANDARD GRATE**

Agave nectar is sweeter than honey but thinner and less cloying, with a mild flavor that showcases the ginger in the marinade. Roasting brings out the sweetness in the accompanying pineapple.

AGAVE-GLAZED CHICKEN THIGHS
with roasted pineapple

INGREDIENTS

2lb (1kg) bone-in, skin-on chicken thighs

1 pineapple, trimmed and cut into 2-in-thick (5-cm) slices

for the marinade

2 cups soy sauce

2 tbsp sesame oil

1 cup agave nectar

¼ cup peeled and minced fresh ginger

2 pineapple slices minced with juice

4 scallions, chopped

2 tbsp minced garlic

2 tbsp toasted sesame seeds

METHOD

1 To make the marinade, in a large bowl, combine all the marinade ingredients. Place chicken in a large resealable plastic bag and add enough marinade to coat. Refrigerate for 2 hours or overnight.

2 In a separate large resealable plastic bag, place sliced pineapple and enough marinade to coat. Refrigerate for 2 hours or overnight.

3 On the stovetop in a small saucepan over medium-high heat, heat the remaining marinade until reduced and slightly thickened, about 10 to 15 minutes.

4 Preheat the grill to 425°F (218°C) using indirect heat with a standard grate and a drip pan installed. Remove chicken and pineapple from the marinade, place on the grate, and close the lid. Roast until the internal temperature reaches 165°F (74°C) and the skin begins to crisp and pineapple begins to caramelize, about 30 to 40 minutes, brushing with the thickened sauce every 10 to 15 minutes.

5 Remove chicken and pineapple from the grill, place on a large serving platter, and let rest for 5 to 10 minutes before serving.

 If you've never had agave before, add it a little at a time to the marinade and test the taste along the way. You can add more or less than the recommended 1 cup depending on your preference.

PREP TIME
1 HR

COOK TIME
60-90 MINS

SERVES
12

HEAT
**DIRECT
350°F (177°C)**

COOKING SURFACE
**CAST IRON GRATE
DUTCH OVEN**

Slowly adding ingredients to a Dutch oven gives each item time to integrate its flavors into the larger dish. Duck renders much like pork, becoming more tender and juicy as it cooks.

DUCK & POTATOES
with roasted salsa verde

INGREDIENTS

8 duck breasts, about 4lb (1.8kg) in total

8 mild green chile peppers

4 tbsp olive oil

kosher salt and freshly ground black pepper

1 large white onion, chopped

1 tbsp cumin seeds

15 tomatillos, husked, rinsed, and cut into wedges

1 cup chicken stock

2 tsp dried oregano

1lb (450g) Yukon Gold potatoes, peeled and cut into cubes

chopped fresh cilantro, to garnish

for the brine

½ cup kosher salt

½ cup packed light brown sugar

3 tbsp pickling spice

6 cups hot water

for the salsa verde

2 cups chicken stock

5 tomatillos, husked, rinsed, and cut into wedges

1 bunch of scallions, coarsely chopped

1½ cups packed fresh cilantro leaves and tender stems

6 garlic cloves, peeled

METHOD

1 To make the brine, in a medium bowl, whisk together salt, brown sugar, pickling spice, and water until salt and sugar have dissolved. Add ice cubes a few at a time until the liquid is no longer hot. Place duck breasts in a resealable plastic bag and add brine to cover. (Any extra brine can be refrigerated and saved for a later use.) Refrigerate for 1 hour.

2 Preheat the grill to 350°F (177°C) using direct heat with a cast iron grate installed and a Dutch oven on the grate. Place green chiles on the grate around the Dutch oven, close the grill lid, and grill until charred, about 7 to 10 minutes. Remove from the grill, seed, dice, and set aside.

3 In the hot Dutch oven, heat oil until shimmering. Remove duck from the brine, pat dry with paper towels, and slice into thin strips. Sprinkle duck with salt and pepper to taste. Working in two batches, add duck to the Dutch oven. Leave the lid off the Dutch oven, close the grill lid, and cook until browned, about 4 minutes per batch, turning occasionally. Using a slotted spoon, transfer duck to a serving bowl, retaining 1 tbsp fat.

4 Add onion to the Dutch oven and sauté until soft, about 5 minutes. Add cumin seeds and cook until onion is golden and cumin is toasted, about 2 minutes. Add tomatillos and cook until tender and browned in spots, about 8 minutes, stirring occasionally.

5 To make the salsa verde, in a blender or food processor, purée all the salsa ingredients until smooth. Return duck and any juices to the Dutch oven. Add 2 cups salsa verde, chicken stock, chiles, and oregano. Place the lid on the Dutch oven, close the grill lid, and simmer until duck is tender, about 2 hours.

6 Add potatoes to the Dutch oven. Replace the lid, close the grill lid, and simmer until potatoes are tender, about 30 minutes. Stir in remaining salsa verde and bring to a simmer. Thin with more stock (if desired), and season with salt and pepper to taste. Sprinkle with cilantro before serving.

PREP TIME
24 HRS

COOK TIME
2½ HRS

SERVES
21

HEAT
INDIRECT 250°F (121°C)

COOKING SURFACE
**CAST IRON GRATE
MULTI-TIERED RACK**

With a chipotle and honey glaze, these chicken wings get spicy.
But an avocado crema—which has the look and feel of guacamole—
will tame the heat. And these wings come with their own pickles!

ADOBO CHICKEN WINGS
with pickled bell peppers

INGREDIENTS

42 chicken wings, about 5lb
(2.3kg) in total

3 cups rice flour

3 tbsp ancho chili powder

3 tsp kosher salt

6 tbsp chopped fresh cilantro,
for garnish

for the pickles

¼ cup sugar

½ cup white vinegar

2 tbsp pickling spice

3 large red bell peppers, cut into
1½-in (3.75-cm) strips

for the glaze

6 chipotle peppers in adobo

3 tbsp adobo sauce

2 cups honey

6 tbsp fresh lime juice

6 tbsp soy sauce

for the crema

2 avocados, halved and pitted

4 tbsp lime juice or to taste

2 cups Mexican crema or sour
cream

kosher salt and freshly ground
black pepper

to smoke

maple or apricot wood chunks

METHOD

1 To make the pickles, in a small saucepan on the stovetop, combine sugar, vinegar, and pickling spice. Bring to a boil over high heat, then reduce heat and simmer for 5 minutes. Bring a separate saucepan of water to boil and blanch the red bell peppers by submerging them in the boiling water for 2 minutes. Pack the peppers in one or two glass jars. Pour the pickling solution over peppers to fill the jars and seal the jars with lids. Refrigerate for at least 1 day.

2 Pat chicken dry with paper towels. Place in a large bowl, sprinkle with rice flour, chili powder, and salt, and toss to coat. Arrange wings in a single layer on a wire rack placed on a baking pan. Refrigerate uncovered for 8 hours.

3 Preheat the grill to 250°F (121°C). Once hot, add the wood chunks and install the heat deflector and a multi-tiered rack. Arrange wings on the rack, close the lid, and smoke until the internal temperature reaches 165°F (74°C), about 2 hours. Remove wings from the grill and let rest for 1 hour.

4 To make the glaze, in a blender, combine peppers, adobo sauce, honey, lime juice, and soy sauce, and purée until smooth. Pour into a small bowl and set aside.

5 Reconfigure the grill for direct heat and install a cast iron grate. Open the top and bottom vents to raise the grill temperature to 400°F (204°C). To make the crema, place avocados cut side down on the grate. Grill until char marks form, about 7 to 10 minutes. Scoop the avocado flesh into a food processor, add lime juice and crema, and process until smooth. Season with salt and pepper to taste.

6 Place wings on the grate and grill until the skin is crisp and grill marks appear, about 2 to 3 minutes per side. Transfer to a serving dish and toss with sauce to coat. Sprinkle with cilantro and serve with the pickles and crema.

PREP TIME **45 MINS**	COOK TIME **8 MINS**	SERVES **8**	HEAT **INDIRECT 400°F (204°C)**	COOKING SURFACE **CAST IRON GRIDDLE**

Savory chicken patties seasoned with garlic and herbs are sandwiched between crisp, buttery waffles and drizzled with sweet-and-spicy syrup. Your brunch guests will thank you.

CHICKEN & WAFFLE SANDWICH
with sriracha maple syrup

INGREDIENTS

for the patties

2lb (1kg) ground chicken

2 tbsp kosher salt

1½ tbsp ground black pepper

1½ tsp paprika

¾ tsp ground cayenne pepper

½ tsp garlic powder

½ tsp onion powder

1 tsp rosemary

1 tsp thyme

1 large egg

½ cup panko breadcrumbs

for the sandwiches

4oz (110g) butter, softened

16 freshly cooked waffles, homemade or frozen

for the syrup

¼ cup maple syrup

2 tbsp sriracha

METHOD

1 Preheat the grill to 400°F (204°C) using indirect heat with a cast iron griddle installed. In a large bowl, combine all the patty ingredients and form into 8 equally sized patties. Set aside.

2 Butter 8 waffles on both sides and place on the griddle, pressing down to ensure they get crispy. Cook until golden brown, about 2 minutes per side. Transfer waffles to a platter and repeat grilling the remaining 8 waffles.

3 To make the syrup, in a small bowl, combine maple syrup and sriracha. Set aside.

4 Place the patties on the griddle, close the lid, and grill until the internal temperature reaches 165°F (74°C), about 3 to 4 minutes per side, flipping once.

5 To assemble the sandwiches, place each patty between two waffles and drizzle with the sriracha maple syrup. Serve immediately.

PREP TIME
4-6 HRS

COOK TIME
90 MINS

SERVES
16

HEAT
**INDIRECT
250°F (121°C)**

COOKING SURFACE
STANDARD GRATE

Brined and smoked chicken creates a flavorful base for this chicken salad, which is dressed with a creamy peanut sauce and studded with crisp cucumber, carrots, and bell pepper.

SMOKED CHICKEN SALAD

INGREDIENTS

1 whole chicken, about 3–4lb (1.4–1.8kg) in total
4 cups shredded napa cabbage
2 carrots, julienned
1 English cucumber, sliced
1 red bell pepper, sliced
kosher salt and freshly ground black pepper
2 scallions, sliced, to garnish
¼ cup crushed peanuts, to garnish

for the dressing

⅓ cup creamy peanut butter
3 tbsp rice vinegar
juice of 1 lime
3 tbsp vegetable oil
2 tsp toasted sesame oil
2 tbsp soy sauce
2 tbsp honey
2 tbsp sugar
1 garlic clove, chopped
1 tbsp chopped fresh ginger
pinch of crushed red pepper flakes
2 tbsp chopped fresh cilantro
kosher salt and freshly ground black pepper

for the brine

½ cup kosher salt
½ cup packed light brown sugar
3 tbsp pickling spice
6 cups hot water

to smoke

apple or cherry wood chunks

METHOD

1 To make the dressing, in a blender or food processor, combine all the dressing ingredients and pulse until smooth and creamy. Season with salt and pepper to taste. Transfer the dressing to an airtight container and refrigerate until needed.

2 To make the brine, in a large bowl, whisk together all the brine ingredients until salt and sugar have dissolved. Add ice cubes a few at a time until the liquid is no longer hot. Place chicken in a large resealable plastic bag and add brine to cover. (Any extra brine can be refrigerated and saved for a later use.) Refrigerate for 4 to 6 hours.

3 Remove chicken from the brine, pat dry with paper towels, and coat with the peanut dressing inside and out. (Reserve remaining dressing and refrigerate.) Let chicken come to room temperature.

4 Preheat the grill to 250°F (121°C). Once hot, add wood chunks and install the heat deflector and a standard grate. Place chicken on the grate, close the lid, and smoke until legs or thighs reach an internal temperature of 170°F (77°C), about 90 minutes. Transfer chicken to a cutting board and let rest for 15 minutes. Once cool, remove chicken meat from the bones and shred. Toss the shredded meat with a few tablespoons of reserved peanut dressing.

5 In a large bowl, combine cabbage, carrots, cucumber, bell pepper, and shredded chicken. Toss with remaining reserved dressing, and season with salt and pepper to taste. Garnish with scallions and peanuts before serving.

 TIP Smoking chicken leaves the meat still somewhat pink, so it's important to make sure the internal temperature reaches 170°F (77°C). This let you know that the meat is fully cooked through.

PREP TIME
30 MINS

COOK TIME
20-30 MINS

SERVES
4

HEAT
**INDIRECT
325°F (163°C)**

COOKING SURFACE
STANDARD GRATE

These juicy chicken breasts are stuffed with a blend of goat cheese, basil, and sun-dried tomatoes and then smoked, melting the cheese and infusing the chicken with an added layer of flavor.

MEDITERRANEAN STUFFED CHICKEN

INGREDIENTS

4 boneless, skinless chicken breasts, about 1½lb (680g) in total

3 tbsp extra virgin olive oil

2 tbsp kosher salt, plus more as needed

2 tbsp ground black pepper, plus more as needed

1 tbsp dried marjoram

for the brine

¼ cup kosher salt

¼ cup packed light brown sugar

2 tbsp pickling spice

3 cups hot water

for the filling

8 sun-dried tomatoes in olive oil, drained and minced

4 basil leaves, stacked, rolled, and cut crosswise into thin strips

4oz (110g) goat cheese, crumbled

kosher salt and freshly ground black pepper

to smoke

apricot, pecan, or wine barrel wood chunks

METHOD

1 To make the brine, in a medium bowl, whisk together salt, brown sugar, pickling spice, and hot water until salt and sugar have dissolved. Add ice cubes a few at a time until the liquid is no longer hot. Place chicken in a large resealable plastic bag and add brine to cover. (Any extra brine can be refrigerated and saved for a later use.) Refrigerate for 30 minutes.

2 To make the filling, in a medium bowl, combine tomatoes, basil, and cheese, and season with salt and pepper to taste.

3 Remove chicken from the brine, pat dry with paper towels, and cut a slit in the side of each chicken breast to create a pocket. Fill the cavities with equal amounts of filling and close up the pockets with toothpicks soaked in water. Lightly coat the breasts with olive oil, and sprinkle with salt, pepper, and marjoram.

4 Preheat the grill to 325°F (163°C). Once hot, add the wood chunks and install the heat deflector and a standard grate. Place chicken on the grate, close the lid, and smoke until chicken reaches an internal temperature of 165°F (74°C), about 20 to 30 minutes.

5 Remove chicken from the grill and serve immediately.

PREP TIME
4–24 HRS

COOK TIME
10 MINS

SERVES
8

HEAT
DIRECT
450°F (232°C)

COOKING SURFACE
CAST IRON GRATE

Inspired by traditional Indonesian grilled chicken recipes, these skewers are coated in an aromatic spice paste that infuses the meat with the flavors of turmeric, ginger, and hot peppers.

SKEWERED BALINESE CHICKEN

INGREDIENTS

10 garlic cloves, peeled

3 fresh cayenne peppers, halved and seeded

3 small shallots, halved

2 fresh bay leaves

1 tbsp chopped fresh ginger

1 tsp ground turmeric

4 tbsp vegetable oil, divided

kosher salt and freshly ground black pepper

2lb (1kg) chicken breast, trimmed and cut into ½-in (1.25-cm) strips

4 limes, halved, to serve

METHOD

1 In a food processor, combine garlic, peppers, shallots, bay leaves, ginger, and turmeric. Pulse until finely chopped. Add 3 tbsp oil and pulse until the mixture forms a paste-like consistency.

2 In a sauté pan on the stovetop, heat remaining 1 tbsp oil over medium heat until shimmering. Add the spice paste, and cook until fragrant and lightly browned, about 5 minutes, stirring often. Remove the skillet from the heat, let the paste cool completely, and season with salt and pepper to taste.

3 Skewer the strips, place in a baking dish, and rub with the paste until thoroughly coated. Cover with plastic wrap and refrigerate for 4 hours or overnight.

4 Preheat the grill to 450°F (232°C) using direct heat with a cast iron grate installed. Place the chicken skewers on the grate, close the lid, and cook for 3 minutes per side. Transfer to a serving dish and squeeze lime juice over top before serving.

TIP Place the cut limes on the grate for a few minutes before squeezing them over the chicken. The heat will help release the juices and make the chicken more flavorful.

PREP TIME **6–24 HRS**	COOK TIME **70–90 MINS**	SERVES **6**	HEAT **INDIRECT** **350ºF (177ºC)**	COOKING SURFACE **STANDARD GRATE** **ROASTING PAN**

Brining a whole chicken allows the brine flavors to penetrate the skin and flesh. But putting butter under and on the skin helps make the chicken skin crispy and the flesh aromatic and juicy.

WHOLE ROASTED CHICKEN
with garlic & fresh herb butter

INGREDIENTS

1 whole chicken, about 5lb (2.3kg) in total

for the brine

½ cup kosher salt

½ cup packed light brown sugar

3 tbsp pickling spice

6 cups hot water

for the butter

3 heads of garlic, separated into peeled cloves

1 tbsp olive oil

8 tbsp unsalted butter, softened

¾ cup chopped mixed fresh herbs, such as thyme, rosemary, and oregano

5 tsp sherry vinegar

2 tbsp kosher salt

METHOD

1 To make the brine, in a large bowl, whisk together all the brine ingredients until salt and sugar have dissolved. Add ice cubes until the liquid is no longer hot. Place chicken in a resealable plastic bag and add brine to cover. (Any extra brine can be refrigerated and saved for a later use.) Refrigerate for 6 to 24 hours.

2 Preheat the grill to 350°F (177°C) using indirect heat with a standard grate installed. Wrap garlic and oil in aluminum foil, place on the grate, close the lid, and cook for 30 minutes. Remove garlic from the grill and roughly chop.

3 To make the butter, in a stand mixer, combine butter, herbs, vinegar, salt, and garlic.

4 Remove chicken from the brine and pat dry with paper towels. Loosen the skin and allow chicken to come to room temperature. Rub butter under the skin and on top of the skin. Reserve remaining butter for basting.

5 Place chicken in a roasting pan breast side up and set the pan on the grate. Close the grill lid and roast until chicken reaches an internal temperature of 170°F (77°C), about 40 to 60 minutes. Baste with more butter every 20 minutes.

6 Remove chicken from the grill, let rest for 10 to 15 minutes, and cut into quarters or carve. Serve with any remaining butter.

TIP Set the chicken on a rack and on top of a can or another container than will withstand being on a grill for an extended period of time. This allows the heat to more evenly surround the chicken.

PREP TIME
1 HR

COOK TIME
1½ HRS

SERVES
10

HEAT
DIRECT
350°F (177°C)

COOKING SURFACE
CAST IRON GRATE
DUTCH OVEN

Traditional Romanian ghiveci features a lot of vegetables cooked with tomatoes to form something similar to French ratatouille. This stew is a perfect pairing for the flavors in grilled chicken.

GRILLED CHICKEN
with ghiveci

INGREDIENTS

8 boneless, skinless chicken thighs, about 2lb (1kg) in total

kosher salt and freshly ground black pepper

2 carrots, peeled

1 red onion, halved

1lb (450g) white or crimini mushrooms

⅔ cup olive oil

5 garlic cloves, chopped

1lb (450g) new potatoes, diced or chopped

28oz (800g) canned San Marzano tomatoes

2 cups chicken stock

2 tbsp mixed herbs, chopped

for the brine

½ cup kosher salt

½ cup packed light brown sugar

3 tbsp pickling spice

6 cups hot water

METHOD

1 To make the brine, in a large bowl, whisk together all the brine ingredients until salt and sugar have dissolved. Add ice cubes a few at a time until the liquid is no longer hot. Place the thighs in a large resealable plastic bag and add brine to cover. (Any extra brine can be refrigerated and saved for a later use.) Refrigerate for 1 hour.

2 Remove chicken from the brine and pat dry with paper towels. Season with salt and pepper to taste, wrap tightly with plastic wrap, and allow to come to room temperature.

3 Preheat the grill to 350°F (177°C) using direct heat with a cast iron grate and a Dutch oven installed. Place carrots, onion, and mushrooms around the Dutch oven, close the grill lid, and grill until softened, about 7 to 10 minutes. Chop carrots and onion, but leave mushrooms whole.

4 In the hot Dutch oven, heat oil until shimmering, and add garlic. With the Dutch oven uncovered, close the grill lid and cook until garlic begins to brown, about 2 minutes. Add carrots, onion, mushrooms, potatoes, tomatoes, and stock to the Dutch oven, and season with salt and pepper to taste. Add mixed herbs, close the grill lid, and cook until the vegetables are tender, about 1 hour.

5 Place chicken thighs on the grate around the Dutch oven, close the grill lid, and grill until tender and slightly charred and the internal temperature reaches 165°F (74°C), about 10 minutes. Add thighs to the Dutch oven with the vegetables. With the Dutch oven uncovered, close the grill lid and cook until chicken is fully cooked, about 10 minutes. Remove the Dutch oven from the grill and serve immediately.

PREP TIME
6–12 HRS

COOK TIME
50 MINS

SERVES
4

HEAT
INDIRECT
375°F (191°C)

COOKING SURFACE
CAST IRON GRATE

The spatchcock technique calls for removing the backbone from a whole chicken and flattening it, increasing the surface area for crisp skin and even cooking. Brining ensures juicy, flavorful meat.

SPATCHCOCKED CHICKEN
with Greek tomato relish

INGREDIENTS

1 whole young chicken, about 4lb (1.8kg) in total, skin on

kosher salt and freshly ground black pepper

for the brine

½ cup kosher salt

½ cup packed light brown sugar

3 tbsp pickling spice

6 cups hot water

for the tomato relish

2 tbsp extra virgin olive oil

1 tbsp red wine vinegar

14.5oz (411g) can diced tomatoes, drained

2 garlic cloves, minced

2 tsp kosher salt

5 basil leaves, chopped

10 Kalamata olives, pitted and chopped

1 small red onion, diced

2oz (55g) dry feta cheese, diced

METHOD

1 To make the brine, in a large bowl, whisk together salt, brown sugar, pickling spice, and water until salt and sugar have dissolved. Add ice cubes a few at a time until the liquid is no longer hot. Place chicken in a large resealable plastic bag and add brine to fully cover. (Any extra brine can be refrigerated and saved for a later use.) Refrigerate for 6 to 12 hours.

2 Remove chicken from the brine and pat dry with paper towels. Place the bird breast side down on a cutting board. Using poultry shears, cut along one side of the backbone, starting at the thigh meat and cutting away from you. Rotate chicken and cut down the opposite side of the backbone. Remove and discard the backbone. Turn chicken breast side up, press firmly on the breastbone to flatten, and tuck the wings behind the back. Rub the skin with salt and pepper to taste.

3 Preheat the grill to 375°F (191°C) using indirect heat with a cast iron grate installed. Place the chicken skin side down on the grate, close the lid, and roast until the internal temperature of the thigh meat reaches 170°F (77°C), about 50 minutes, turning once.

4 To make the tomato relish, in a large bowl, stir together oil, vinegar, tomatoes, garlic, salt, basil, olives, and onion. Gently stir in feta.

5 Transfer the chicken to a platter and let rest for 10 minutes before serving with the tomato relish.

PREP TIME
30 MINS

COOK TIME
10-15 MINS

SERVES
4

HEAT
DIRECT
350°F (177°C)

COOKING SURFACE
CAST IRON GRATE

Grilled chicken pairs well with a variety of fruits, including the deep purple blackberries and ripe nectarines in this recipe. Jalapeño and balsamic vinegar provide balance to the sweet fruits.

GRILLED CHICKEN BREASTS
with nectarine & blackberry salsa

INGREDIENTS

4 skinless, boneless chicken breasts, about 1½lb (680g) in total

kosher salt and freshly ground black pepper

2 nectarines, halved and pitted

1 jalapeño pepper, seeded and minced

2 cups blackberries, roughly chopped

4 tbsp chopped fresh cilantro

2 tbsp balsamic vinegar, plus more to taste

for the brine

¼ cup kosher salt

¼ cup packed light brown sugar

2 tbsp pickling spice

3 cups hot water

METHOD

1 To make the brine, in a medium bowl, whisk together all the brine ingredients until salt and sugar have dissolved. Add ice cubes a few at a time until the liquid is no longer hot. Place chicken in a resealable plastic bag and add the brine to cover. (Any extra brine can be refrigerated and saved for a later use.) Refrigerate for 30 minutes.

2 Remove chicken from the brine, pat dry with paper towels, and season with salt and pepper to taste. Set aside and allow to come to room temperature.

3 Preheat the grill to 350°F (177°C) using direct heat with a cast iron grate installed. Place nectarines on the grate skin side up, close the lid, and grill until softened and slightly charred, about 2 minutes. Remove from the grill and dice.

4 In a medium bowl, combine nectarines, jalapeño, blackberries, and cilantro. Add vinegar and toss to combine, adding more vinegar (if desired).

5 Spoon some of the liquid from the salsa over the chicken breasts and rub into the meat. Place chicken on the grate, close the lid, and grill until the meat reaches an internal temperature of 160°F (71°C), about 4 to 6 minutes per side. Remove chicken from the grill and top with the blackberry salsa before serving.

TIP

Exchange the nectarines and blackberries with other citrus fruits and other seasonal berries. Some others to try include pineapple, oranges, kiwi, mango, strawberries, raspberries, and blueberries.

PREP TIME
25 MINS

COOK TIME
30-35 MINS

SERVES
10

HEAT
**DIRECT
325°F (163°C)**

COOKING SURFACE
**CAST IRON GRATE
DUTCH OVEN**

Wild mushrooms are the star of this French-style dish, which brings together tender pieces of chicken and earthy mushrooms in a creamy, savory sauce. Serve on its own or over fresh pasta.

CHICKEN & MUSHROOM RAGOUT

INGREDIENTS

2½lb boneless, skinless chicken, breasts or thighs, cut into ½-in (1.25-cm) pieces

2 tbsp extra virgin olive oil, divided

kosher salt and freshly ground black pepper

2 tbsp cold unsalted butter, cubed and tossed with flour to coat

½lb (225g) assorted mushrooms (such as oyster, cremini, and stemmed shiitake), thickly sliced

¼ cup finely chopped shallots

2 tsp balsamic vinegar

¼ cup low-sodium chicken stock

⅓ cup crème fraîche or whipping cream

⅓ cup chopped fresh flat-leaf parsley, plus more for serving

METHOD

1 Preheat the grill to 325°F (163°C) using direct heat with a cast iron grate installed and a Dutch oven on the grate. Lightly coat chicken with 1 tbsp oil, and season with salt and pepper to taste (or a favorite rub). Place chicken in the Dutch oven, close the grill lid, and cook chicken until beginning to brown, about 10 to 15 minutes, flipping once.

2 Add butter, mushrooms, and remaining 1 tbsp oil to the Dutch oven, close the grill lid, and cook until mushrooms are tender and brown, about 10 minutes, stirring often. Add shallots and vinegar to the Dutch oven, close the grill lid, and sauté until shallots are tender, about 2 minutes. Season lightly with salt and pepper to taste.

3 Add stock to the Dutch oven, close the grill lid, and simmer for 5 minutes. Stir in crème fraîche and parsley. Season the ragout with salt and pepper to taste. Top with more parsley and serve immediately.

TIP

This recipe depends on quality mushrooms. Make sure the mushrooms you buy are firm, light in color, and hardy in texture. Buying them whole rather than pre-sliced adds to their longevity and viability.

PREP TIME
25 MINS

COOK TIME
15–20 MINS

SERVES
8

HEAT
**DIRECT
425°F (218°C)**

COOKING SURFACE
CAST IRON GRATE

Duck meat is fattier and more flavorful than most poultry, making it a perfect choice for high-heat searing. The tangy, garnet-hued sauce is a beautiful complement to the rich, succulent meat.

SEARED DUCK
with huckleberry sauce

INGREDIENTS

2lb (1kg) skin-on duck breasts

¼ cup scallions, thinly sliced, to garnish

for the marinade

1 cup huckleberries, fresh or frozen

1 bunch of scallions, thinly sliced

½ bunch of fresh cilantro

2 garlic cloves, chopped

1 tsp finely grated lime zest

1 tsp finely grated orange zest

¼ cup fresh lime juice

¼ cup fresh orange juice

¼ cup low-sodium soy sauce

2 tbsp vegetable oil

2 tbsp kosher salt

METHOD

1 To make the marinade, in a food processor, combine all the sauce ingredients and pulse until a purée forms. Reserve ¼ cup marinade and place the remainder in a large resealable bag. Add duck breasts to the bag, turning to coat. Refrigerate for 20 minutes.

2 While duck marinates, preheat the grill to 425°F (218°C) using direct heat with a cast iron grate installed. Remove duck breasts from the marinade and place skin side down on the grate. Close the lid and grill until lightly brown, about 5 to 8 minutes. Flip breasts and grill until an instant-read thermometer inserted into the thickest part of a breast reads 165°F (74°C), about 10 to 12 minutes more.

3 Remove duck breasts from the grill, and serve immediately with the reserved ¼ cup marinade and sliced scallions.

TIP

If huckleberries are unavailable, substitute an equal amount of blackberries or black raspberries to achieve a similar tangy flavor and deep color.

PREP TIME
1 HR

COOK TIME
35–45 MINS

SERVES
4

HEAT
**INDIRECT
170°F (77°C)**

COOKING SURFACE
CAST IRON GRATE

Contrasting spices abound in this recipe—from making your own BBQ sauce with Tabasco and brown sugar to submerging the legs in a sweet–salty brine to coating them with an ancho powder mix.

BBQ CHICKEN QUARTERS

INGREDIENTS

4 skin-on, bone-in chicken
  leg quarters

for the brine

½ cup kosher salt

½ cup packed light brown sugar

3 tbsp pickling spice

6 cups hot water

for the sauce

¼ cup molasses

2 cups ketchup

3 tsp Worcestershire sauce

2 tbsp lemon juice

½ tsp Tabasco sauce

⅜ cup packed dark brown sugar

½ tsp ground cayenne pepper

2 garlic cloves, finely minced

1 tbsp ground black pepper

for the rub

4 tbsp kosher salt

4 tbsp ground black pepper

2 tbsp ancho powder

METHOD

1 To make the brine, in a medium bowl, whisk together salt, brown sugar, pickling spice, and water until salt and sugar have dissolved. Add ice cubes a few at a time until the liquid is no longer hot. Place chicken in a resealable plastic bag and add brine to cover. (Any extra brine can be refrigerated and saved for a later use.) Refrigerate for 1 hour.

2 To make the BBQ sauce, in a small saucepan, combine all the sauce ingredients. Place the saucepan on the stovetop over medium heat and simmer for 15 minutes, stirring occasionally. Remove from the heat and set aside.

3 To make the rub, in a small bowl, combine salt, pepper, and ancho powder. Remove chicken from the brine, pat dry with paper towels, and season with some of the rub mixture. Let chicken come to room temperature.

4 Preheat the grill to 425°F (218°C) using indirect heat with a cast iron grate installed. Brush chicken with the BBQ sauce and place on the grate. Close the lid and grill until the internal temperature reaches 170°F (77°C), 20 to 30 minutes, turning to evenly crisp the skin. Brush chicken with the BBQ sauce every 10 minutes while cooking.

5 Remove chicken from the grill and season with more rub mixture to taste. Let rest for 10 minutes. Serve with the remaining BBQ sauce.

PREP TIME
6–24 HRS

COOK TIME
2 HRS

SERVES
10

HEAT
**INDIRECT
275°F (135°C)**

COOKING SURFACE
STANDARD GRATE

This recipe has many different components that take some time to prepare, but they all come together to create shredded chicken that's perfect for sandwiches or tacos or an addition to salads.

SWEET & SPICY PULLED CHICKEN

INGREDIENTS

2 whole chickens, about 4lb
 (1.8kg) each

for the brine

½ cup kosher salt

½ cup packed light brown sugar

3 tbsp pickling spice

6 cups hot water

for the rub

4 tbsp paprika

2 tbsp ground black pepper

4 tsp ground cayenne pepper

2 tbsp raw sugar

2 tbsp kosher salt

for the sauce

1 cup bourbon

4 tbsp molasses

3 cups cider vinegar

2 cups water

4 chipotle peppers in adobo sauce,
 chopped

4 tbsp kosher salt

2 tbsp crushed red pepper flakes

2 tbsp ground black pepper

4 tsp ground cayenne pepper

to smoke

peach, plum, or grapevine
 wood chunks

METHOD

1 To make the brine, in a large bowl, whisk together all the brine ingredients until salt and sugar have dissolved. Add ice cubes a few at a time until the liquid is no longer hot. Place each chicken in a resealable plastic bag and add brine to cover. (Any extra brine can be refrigerated and saved for a later use.) Refrigerate for 6 to 24 hours.

2 To make the rub, in a small bowl, combine all the rub ingredients. Remove chicken from the brine and pat dry with paper towels. Cover all the surfaces with the rub, wrap tightly with plastic wrap, and allow to come to room temperature.

3 To make the sauce, in a large saucepan, combine all the sauce ingredients. Place pan on the stovetop over high heat, bring to a simmer, and cook for 5 minutes.

4 Preheat the grill to 275°F (135°C). Once hot, add the wood chunks and install the heat deflector and a standard grate. Place chicken on the grate breast side up, close the lid, and smoke until the meat of the thigh reaches an internal temperature of 170°F (77°C), about 60 to 90 minutes, basting with sauce every 15 to 20 minutes. Remove chicken from the grill and let rest for 20 minutes.

5 On the stovetop in a small saucepan over high heat, boil any remaining basting sauce for 5 minutes. Remove the meat from the bones and shred. Toss the shredded chicken with the warmed basting sauce and serve immediately.

PREP TIME
5-26 HRS

COOK TIME
3 HRS

SERVES
6

HEAT
**INDIRECT
275°F (135°C)**

COOKING SURFACE
STANDARD GRATE

Cherry wood imparts a lightly fruity and sweet smoke, bringing out deeper flavors in the turkey. Chill and purée the glaze before use for a smoother and more even texture—and crisper skin.

CHERRY-SMOKED TURKEY LEGS
with maple & cranberry glaze

INGREDIENTS

4 whole turkey legs, about 2.5lb (1.4kg) each

kosher salt and freshly ground black pepper

for the brine

½ cup kosher salt

½ cup packed light brown sugar

3 tbsp pickling spice

6 cups hot water

for the glaze

12oz (340g) fresh or frozen cranberries

1 tbsp grated fresh ginger

1 tsp ground cloves

1½ cups maple syrup

1 cup water

to smoke

cherry, peach, or apple wood chunks

METHOD

1 To make the brine, in a large bowl, whisk together salt, brown sugar, pickling spice, and water until salt and sugar have dissolved. Add ice cubes until the liquid is no longer hot. Place turkey legs in two large resealable plastic bags and add brine to cover. Refrigerate for 3 to 24 hours. Before grilling, remove turkey from the brine, pat dry with paper towels, and refrigerate uncovered for 2 hours. (Any extra brine can be refrigerated and saved for a later use.)

2 Preheat the grill to 275°F (135°C). Once hot, add the wood chunks and install the heat deflector and a standard grate. Remove turkey legs from the fridge and let come to room temperature.

3 To make the glaze, in a medium saucepan, combine cranberries, ginger, cloves, syrup, and water. Place the saucepan on the stovetop over medium heat and bring to a gentle boil. Cook until the cranberry skins burst and the mixture thickens, about 10 to 15 minutes. Don't overcook to the point where the syrup begins to smell like scorched sugar.

4 Place turkey legs on the grate, close the lid, and smoke for 1 hour. After 1 hour, brush with glaze every 15 minutes until the meat reaches an internal temperature of 180°F (82°C) degrees, about 1 to 2 more hours.

5 Remove turkey legs from the grill, let rest for 15 minutes, and slice. Serve with any remaining glaze.

PREP TIME
2-24 HRS

COOK TIME
15-20 MINS

SERVES
10

HEAT
DIRECT
400°F (204°C)

COOKING SURFACE
CAST IRON GRATE

These salty—sweet chicken skewers are coated with a rich glaze that features orange juice, garlic, shallots, and ginger. Grilling caramelizes the glaze, creating a crisp exterior and tender meat.

SESAME CHICKEN SKEWERS
with citrus & ginger glaze

INGREDIENTS

2½lb (1.2kg) boneless, skinless chicken thighs, cut into 1-in (2.5-cm) cubes

2 tbsp fish sauce

1 tbsp light brown sugar

1 tbsp orange juice

¼ cup white sesame seeds

¼ cup black sesame seeds

⅓ cup sliced almonds

2 scallions, thinly sliced

for the brine

½ cup kosher salt

½ cup packed light brown sugar

3 tbsp pickling spice

6 cups hot water

for the glaze

⅔ cup packed light brown sugar

⅓ cup Asian fish sauce

⅓ cup orange juice

⅓ cup rice vinegar

2 tbsp honey

4 medium garlic cloves, minced

2 medium shallots, chopped

1-in (2.5-cm) piece fresh ginger, peeled and minced

METHOD

1 To make the brine, in a large bowl, whisk together salt, brown sugar, pickling spice, and hot water until salt and sugar have dissolved. Add ice cubes a few at a time until the liquid is no longer hot. Place chicken in the brine, cover with plastic wrap, and refrigerate for 45 minutes. (Any extra brine can be refrigerated and saved for a later use.)

2 Remove chicken from the brine and place in a large resealable plastic bag. Add fish sauce, sugar, and orange juice, shaking well to coat, and refrigerate for 2 hours or overnight.

3 To make the glaze, in a medium saucepan, combine sugar, fish sauce, orange juice, vinegar, and honey, and place the pan on the stovetop over medium heat. Stir until sugar dissolves. Add garlic, shallots, and ginger, and continue to cook until the glaze is thick and sticky and easily coats the back of a spoon, about 5 to 10 minutes, stirring occasionally. Remove the glaze from the heat and set aside.

4 Preheat the grill to 400°F (204°F) using direct heat with a cast iron grate installed. Thread the chicken cubes onto wooden skewers, place on the grate, and close the lid. Cook until fully cooked and crispy, about 8 minutes, turning and brushing with glaze several times.

5 Remove the skewers from the grill and sprinkle with sesame seeds, almonds, and scallions. Serve immediately.

PREP TIME
32–34 HRS

COOK TIME
7 HRS

SERVES
12

HEAT
INDIRECT
325°F (163°C)

COOKING SURFACE
STANDARD GRATE

This could be the last turkey recipe you need. Incredibly moist with beautifully browned skin, it's the perfect centerpiece for any holiday table. Don't cut the brine time—it's the key to success.

ROASTED TURKEY
with citrus & fresh herbs

INGREDIENTS

1 whole turkey, about 20lb (9kg) in total

for the brine

1 tbsp mustard seed

2 whole star anise

¼ cup black peppercorns

12 whole juniper berries

3 gallons (11.5 liters) water

3 cups kosher salt

½ cup packed light brown sugar

2 limes, sliced

2 lemons, sliced

3 oranges, halved

1 green apple, sliced

1 head of garlic, halved horizontally

1 bunch of fresh flat-leaf parsley

1 bunch of fresh thyme

6 sprigs of fresh rosemary

METHOD

1 To make the brine, on the stovetop in a heavy-bottomed stockpot over medium-high heat, toast mustard seed, star anise, peppercorns, and juniper berries until mustard seed is golden brown and spices are fragrant, about 5 minutes. Add 1½ gallons (5.7 liters) water and the remaining brine ingredients to the pot, and heat until the water simmers and salt and sugar dissolve, about 5 minutes. Remove the pot from the heat, add the remaining 1½ gallons (5.7 liters) water, and refrigerate uncovered until fully chilled, about 4 hours. (Any extra brine can be refrigerated and saved for a later use.)

2 Using a meat injector, inject turkey with the brine, starting with the breast meat and moving outward. Continue until the flesh begins to feel plump and firm. Place turkey in a 5-gallon (11.5-liter) plastic bucket and add brine to completely submerge. Cover and refrigerate for 24 hours.

3 Remove turkey from the brine, rinse with cold water, and pat dry with paper towels. Strain out the solid pieces of fruit, herbs, and spices from the brine, and place them in the cavity of the bird. Allow the bird to sit uncovered at room temperature until the skin is sticky to the touch, about 4 to 6 hours. (This aids in the cooked color and crispiness of the skin.)

4 Preheat the grill to 325°F (163°C) using indirect heat. Place an aluminum drip pan filled with water or stock on the heat deflector and install a standard grate. Place turkey on the grate, close the lid, and roast until the internal temperature reaches 160°F (71°C) in the breast meat and 170°F (77°C) in the dark meat, about 15 to 20 minutes per pound (approximately 30 to 40 minutes per kilogram).

5 Transfer turkey to a serving platter, tent with aluminum foil, and let rest for 15 to 30 minutes before carving and serving.

SEAFOOD

PREP TIME
40 MINS

COOK TIME
20 MINS

SERVES
6

HEAT
**DIRECT
400°F (204°C)**

COOKING SURFACE
CAST IRON GRATE

Whole grilled fish is not only impressive to serve, but it's also remarkably delicious. Stuffed with aromatics, this fish is moist, flaky, and delicately flavored with lemon, garlic, and herbs.

GRILLED RED SNAPPER
with tomato & onion sauce

INGREDIENTS

2 whole red snapper, about 4lb (1.8kg) in total

kosher salt and freshly ground black pepper

3 lemons, thinly sliced, plus more lemon wedges to serve

4 garlic cloves, peeled

2-in (5-cm) piece fresh ginger, peeled and thinly sliced

a few sprigs of fresh oregano

a few sprigs of fresh flat-leaf parsley, plus leaves to garnish

2 tbsp extra virgin olive oil

for the sauce

½ cup extra virgin olive oil, plus more for grilling

2 medium garlic cloves

2 red onions, halved

4 Roma tomatoes, roughly chopped

2 tsp minced fresh oregano

METHOD

1 Preheat the grill to 400°F (204°C) using direct heat with a cast iron grate installed. Brush onion halves with oil, place on the grate, close the lid, and grill until beginning to soften and char, about 4 to 6 minutes. Remove from the grill, let cool slightly, and roughly chop.

2 To make the sauce, in a food processor, combine oil, garlic, and half the onions, and pulse until they form a coarse paste. Add tomatoes and oregano, and pulse briefly until the sauce has a chunky, salsa-like consistency. Transfer to a bowl and stir in reserved onion. Season with black pepper to taste and set aside.

3 Remove fish from the fridge and let come to room temperature. Thoroughly pat dry with paper towels, then season inside and out with salt and pepper to taste. Stuff with lemon slices, garlic, ginger slices, and oregano and parsley sprigs. Rub the exterior with oil.

4 Place fish on the grate, close the lid, and grill until the bottom sides brown, about 5 minutes. Using a spatula, carefully attempt to lift the fish from below. If they resist, allow them to cook for 1 minute more and try again. When fish lift easily from the grill, flip and continue to grill until fish begin to flake and an instant-read thermometer inserted in the thickest part reads 135°F (57°C), about 7 to 10 minutes.

5 Transfer to a serving platter and let rest for 5 minutes. Spoon the tomato sauce over top, and garnish with freshly chopped parsley. Serve with lemon wedges.

PREP TIME
60-90 MINS

COOK TIME
55-75 MINS

SERVES
8

HEAT
INDIRECT
225ºF (107ºC)

COOKING SURFACE
CAST IRON GRATE
CAST IRON SKILLET

Brining your salmon before smoking helps to deepen the fish's natural flavors while taking on the sweet—salty brining spices. A vibrant, nutty pesto brings even more flavor to the salmon.

SMOKED KING SALMON
with walnut pesto

INGREDIENTS

2lb (1kg) skinless King salmon fillets

for the brine
½ cup kosher salt

½ cup packed light brown sugar

3 tbsp pickling spice

6 cups hot water

for the pesto
5 tbsp extra virgin olive oil, divided

¼ cup walnut halves

2 cups baby arugula, loosely packed

1 cup fresh basil leaves, loosely packed

3 tbsp freshly grated Parmigiano-Reggiano

1 garlic clove

kosher salt and freshly ground black pepper

to smoke
alder or cedar wood chunks

METHOD

1 To make the brine, in a medium bowl, whisk together salt, brown sugar, pickling spice, and water until salt and sugar have dissolved. Add ice cubes until the liquid is no longer hot. Place salmon in a resealable plastic bag, add the brine to cover, and refrigerate for 30 minutes. (Any extra brine can be refrigerated and saved for a later use.)

2 Remove salmon from the brine, pat dry with paper towels, and refrigerate until the surface begins to look dry and feel slightly tacky, about 30 to 60 minutes more.

3 Preheat the grill to 225°F (107°C) using indirect heat. Once hot, add the wood chunks and install a cast iron grate and a cast iron skillet. Place 1 tbsp oil and walnuts in the skillet, close the lid, and cook until they just begin to toast, about 10 to 15 minutes. Remove the walnuts from the grill and let cool.

4 To make the pesto, in a food processor, combine walnuts, arugula, basil, Parmigiano-Reggiano, and garlic. Process until the mixture is finely chopped. With the processor running, slowly add 4 tbsp oil until well combined. Thin the pesto with 1 tbsp water (if desired). Transfer to a bowl and season with salt and pepper to taste.

5 Place salmon on the grate, close the lid, and cook until the fish reaches an internal temperature of 135°F (57°C) and just begins to flake, about 45 to 60 minutes. Remove salmon from the grill, and serve immediately with the pesto.

PREP TIME
1 HR

COOK TIME
15 MINS

SERVES
4

HEAT
INDIRECT
400°F (204°C)

COOKING SURFACE
STANDARD GRATE
CAST IRON SKILLET

This take on a Chesapeake Bay classic is mostly faithful to the traditional recipe, but a remoulade made with horseradish and sriracha turns ordinary tarter sauce into a spicy condiment.

MARYLAND CRAB CAKES
with horseradish & sriracha remoulade

INGREDIENTS

½ cup crushed saltine crackers

1 tsp mustard

½ tbsp Old Bay Seasoning

¼ tsp kosher salt

1 large egg, beaten

2 tbsp mayonnaise

½ tsp Worcestershire sauce

1lb (450g) fresh lump crabmeat, such as blue crab

1 tbsp chopped fresh flat-leaf parsley

1 tbsp canola oil

1 tbsp unsalted butter, melted

for the remoulade

½ cup mayonnaise

1 tbsp prepared horseradish

1 tbsp sriracha

1 tbsp capers

1 tbsp apple cider vinegar

1 tbsp lemon juice

2 tsp Dijon mustard

1 shallot, coarsely chopped

METHOD

1 To make the remoulade, in a food processor, combine mayonnaise, horseradish, sriracha, capers, vinegar, lemon juice, mustard, and shallot until smooth. Pour mixture into a small bowl, cover with plastic wrap, and refrigerate until ready to serve.

2 In a small bowl, combine crackers, mustard, Old Bay Seasoning, and salt. In a large bowl, combine egg, mayonnaise, and Worcestershire sauce. Fold in the cracker mixture, and add crabmeat and parsley. Shape the mixture into small cakes, ensuring not to break up the crabmeat, and refrigerate for 1 hour. (This will prevent the cakes from falling apart while cooking.)

3 Preheat the grill to 400°F (204°C) using indirect heat with the heat deflector and a cast iron skillet installed. Place oil and butter in the skillet, add the crab cakes to the skillet, close the lid, and cook until golden brown and the internal temperature reaches 140°F (60°C), about 15 minutes, flipping halfway through.

4 Remove the crab cakes from the grill. Serve immediately or keep warm in a 200°F (93°C) oven, and top with the remoulade.

TIP

To give your crab cakes a smoky flavor, add wood chunks to the coals once the grill has come up to temperature. Some good woods to use include apple and hickory.

PREP TIME
20 MINS

COOK TIME
8-12 MINS

SERVES
4

HEAT
DIRECT
450°F (232°C)

COOKING SURFACE
CAST IRON GRATE

A spicy Cajun seasoning blend coats this flaky white fish, which is complemented by a creamy, sweet-and-tangy sauce. Served on a robust hoagie roll, it makes a satisfying lunch.

BLACKENED GROUPER SANDWICH

INGREDIENTS

4 skinless grouper fillets,
  about 6oz (170g) each
2 tbsp canola oil

for the sauce
¼ cup mayonnaise
1½ tbsp sweet pickle relish
1 tbsp coarse ground mustard
1 tbsp ketchup

for the seasoning
2 tsp onion powder
2 tsp garlic powder
2 tsp dried oregano
2 tsp dried basil
1½ tsp dried thyme
1½ tsp ground black pepper
1½ tsp ground white pepper
1½ tsp ground cayenne pepper
5 tsp paprika
3 tsp kosher salt

to serve
4 hoagie rolls
baby arugula
tomato slices
pickle spears

METHOD

1 Preheat the grill to 450°F (232°C) using direct heat with a cast iron grate installed and a cast iron skillet on the grate.

2 To make the sauce, in a medium bowl, combine mayonnaise, relish, mustard, and ketchup. Refrigerate until ready to serve.

3 To make the seasoning, in a small bowl, combine all the seasoning ingredients. Coat the fish fillets on all sides with the seasoning.

4 In the hot skillet, heat oil until shimmering. Place fish fillets in the skillet, close the lid, and cook until fish begin to form a crust, slightly char, and begin to flake, about 3 to 4 minutes per side.

5 Cut rolls in half, place on the grate, close the lid, and grill until grill marks appear, about 2 to 3 minutes.

6 Spread the sauce on the rolls. Place a fillet on each bottom bun, top with arugula and tomato, and close sandwiches. Serve immediately.

TIP If grouper is unavailable, you can substitute another firm-fleshed white fish. Cod, halibut, and catfish are all good choices.

PREP TIME
20 MINS

COOK TIME
7–12 MINS

SERVES
4

HEAT
**INDIRECT
400°F (204°C)**

COOKING SURFACE
CAST IRON SKILLET

In traditional New Orleans style, these juicy jumbo shrimp are simmered in a savory sauce and served dripping with butter. Have plenty of crusty bread—and napkins—on hand to soak up the sauce.

CREOLE BBQ SHRIMP

INGREDIENTS

½ cup Worcestershire sauce

2 tbsp fresh lemon juice

2 tsp ground black pepper

1 tsp minced garlic

12 jumbo shrimp, about 1½lb (680g) in total, heads on and unpeeled

1¼ cup cold unsalted butter, cut into cubes

kosher salt

crusty French bread, to serve

for the seasoning

1 tbsp onion powder

1 tbsp garlic powder

1 tbsp dried oregano

1 tbsp dried basil

1½ tsp dried thyme

1½ tsp ground black pepper

1½ tsp ground white pepper

1½ tsp ground cayenne pepper

2½ tbsp paprika

1½ tbsp kosher salt

to smoke

apple, pecan, or hickory wood chunks

5 sprigs of fresh rosemary

METHOD

1 Preheat the grill to 400°F (204°C). Once hot, add the wood chunks and rosemary sprigs to the coals. Install the heat deflector and place a cast iron skillet on top.

2 In a medium bowl, combine all the seasoning ingredients. (This makes 10 tbsp Creole seasoning blend. Any extra seasoning can be stored in an airtight container for up to 3 months.)

3 In the hot skillet, combine Worcestershire sauce, lemon juice, pepper, garlic, and 2 tbsp Creole seasoning. Close the grill lid and cook until the liquid begins to simmer, about 2 minutes, then add shrimp. Close the grill lid and cook shrimp until opaque, about 5 to 10 minutes.

4 Remove the skillet from the grill and scatter the butter over top. Gently stir until butter has melted, and season with salt to taste. Serve immediately with crusty French bread.

TIP

Although unpeeled jumbo shrimp will have the best flavor, you can also use smaller peeled shrimp. Just reduce the cook time to 3 to 5 minutes.

PREP TIME
20 MINS

COOK TIME
20-25 MINS

SERVES
8

HEAT
**DIRECT
500°F (260°C)**

COOKING SURFACE
CAST IRON GRIDDLE

Grilled scallops are complemented by a beurre blanc—French for "white butter"—that matches the creamy taste of the scallops. The raspberries give the buttery sauce a pink hue and tart flavor.

SEARED SCALLOPS
with raspberry beurre blanc

INGREDIENTS

2 tbsp olive oil

1 tbsp unsalted butter

24 sea scallops, U-10

kosher salt and freshly ground white pepper

for the beurre blanc

½ cup white wine

1 tsp ground black pepper

4 sprigs of fresh thyme

¼ cup rice wine vinegar

1 cup fresh raspberries

1 shallot, minced

½ cup heavy cream

½ cup cold unsalted butter, cut into cubes

1 tbsp soy sauce, plus more as desired

METHOD

1 To make the beurre blanc, in a medium saucepan, combine wine, pepper, thyme, vinegar, raspberries, and shallot, and place on the stovetop over medium heat. Simmer until reduced to a thin layer of liquid on the bottom of the pot, about 10 minutes. Add cream, and reduce until it has cooked down to a thin layer again, about 5 to 7 minutes. Slowly add butter, stirring constantly. Taste and season with salt, pepper, and soy sauce.

2 Preheat the grill to 500°F (260°C) using direct heat with a cast iron griddle installed. Add oil and butter to the griddle. Once butter has melted, place scallops on the griddle, close the lid, and sear until brown on top and bottom, about 2 to 4 minutes each side.

3 Remove scallops from the grill and divide evenly among serving plates. Spoon warm beurre blanc over top. Serve immediately.

The designation "U-10" means a pound of scallops has 10 or fewer scallops. For this recipe, you need about 3lb (1.4kg) of scallops, and if you end up with more than 24 scallops, no one should complain.

PREP TIME
20 MINS

COOK TIME
40 MINS

SERVES
12

HEAT
**DIRECT
425°F (220°C)**

COOKING SURFACE
**CAST IRON GRATE
DUTCH OVEN**

A silky, creamy cheese sauce with a rich, smoky flavor coats this decadent pasta dish. Use the seafood of your choice: shrimp, scallops, or any flaky white fish—or a combination of all three.

SEAFOOD & SMOKED GOUDA PASTA

INGREDIENTS

1 red bell pepper, halved

4 asparagus stalks

8 tbsp olive oil

8 garlic cloves, minced

2lb (1kg) raw seafood, such as shrimp, scallops, or white fish, thawed if frozen

kosher salt and freshly ground black pepper

16oz (450g) dried vermicelli

crushed red pepper flakes, to garnish

chopped fresh flat-leaf parsley, to garnish

for the sauce

2 cups heavy cream

½ cup unsalted butter, softened

½ cup grated smoked gouda

freshly ground black pepper

METHOD

1 Preheat the grill to 350°F (177°C) using direct heat with a cast iron grate installed and a Dutch oven on the grate. Place pepper and asparagus on the grate (not in the Dutch oven), close the grill lid, and grill until beginning to soften and char, about 7 to 10 minutes. Remove from the grill, chop, and set aside.

2 To the hot Dutch oven, add olive oil and garlic. Cook until fragrant, about 30 seconds. Add seafood, season well with salt and pepper, and close the grill lid. Cook until seafood has begun to look opaque and take on color, about 5 minutes, stirring once. Transfer the cooked seafood to a cutting board and return the Dutch oven to the grill. Cut seafood into bite-sized pieces. Set aside.

3 To make the sauce, add cream and butter to the hot Dutch oven, and whisk gently until butter has melted. Sprinkle in smoked gouda, and stir to incorporate. Season with freshly ground black pepper to taste. Close the grill lid and reduce the cream sauce until just thickened, about 10 minutes, stirring occasionally.

4 On the stovetop, cook vermicelli according to package directions until cooked but still firm to the bite. Drain briefly in a colander.

5 Add seafood, pasta, and vegetables to the Dutch oven. Gently toss to coat with the sauce. Garnish with crushed red pepper flakes and parsley. Serve immediately.

PREP TIME
30 MINS

COOK TIME
40-55 MINS

SERVES
4

HEAT
**INDIRECT
400°F (204°C)**

COOKING SURFACE
**CAST IRON GRATE
DUTCH OVEN**

Tender and deeply flavorful, these scallops are prepared in a salt pack, which infuses them with flavor and readies them for smoking. Their decadent smokiness is complemented by a savory couscous pilaf.

SMOKED SCALLOPS
with grilled vegetable couscous

INGREDIENTS

¼ tsp ground coriander

½ tsp ground white pepper

¼ tsp ground cloves

3 tbsp sugar

2 cups kosher salt

3 tbsp chopped fresh cilantro

2 tbsp finely grated lemon zest

12 large sea scallops

for the couscous

½ red bell pepper

2 Roma tomatoes

1 medium red onion, halved

¼ cup balsamic vinegar

½ tsp Dijon mustard

1 garlic clove, coarsely chopped

½ cup olive oil, plus 2 tbsp

kosher salt and freshly ground black pepper

1½ cups dried Israeli couscous

3 cups vegetable stock, warmed

4 basil leaves, stacked, rolled, and cut crosswise into thin strips

¼ cup chopped fresh flat-leaf parsley

to smoke

alder, grapevine, or pecan wood chunks

METHOD

1 In a large bowl, combine coriander, white pepper, cloves, sugar, salt, cilantro, and lemon zest. Bury scallops in the spice mixture, cover with plastic wrap, and refrigerate for 30 minutes.

2 Preheat the grill to 400°F (204°C) using indirect heat with a cast iron grate installed and a Dutch oven on the grate. Place pepper, tomatoes, and onion on the grate around the Dutch oven and cook until beginning to soften and char, about 7 to 10 minutes. Transfer the vegetables to a cutting board and dice.

3 In a large bowl, whisk together vinegar, mustard, and garlic. Slowly add ½ cup olive oil and whisk until combined. Season well with salt and pepper. Add the diced grilled vegetables and toss to coat. Set aside to marinate at room temperature for 15 minutes.

4 To the hot Dutch oven, heat the remaining 2 tbsp oil until shimmering. Add couscous and toast until lightly golden brown, about 2 minutes. Add stock to cover, close grill, and cook uncovered until couscous is cooked but still firm to the bite and the liquid is absorbed, about 10 minutes. Add the cooked couscous to the bowl with the grilled vegetables and toss well to incorporate. Set aside.

5 Convert the grill for smoking by removing the cast iron grate, adding one wood chunk to the hot coals, and installing the heat deflector and a standard grate. Close the top and bottom vents most of the way to reduce the temperature to 225°F (107°C).

6 Remove the scallops from the salt pack, rinse under cold water, and pat dry with paper towels. Place scallops on the grate and smoke until slightly firm and light brown in color, about 20 to 30 minutes. Just before serving, scatter the basil and parsley over the couscous and lightly toss. Serve the scallops immediately on a bed of couscous.

PREP TIME
20 MINS

COOK TIME
12-20 MINS

SERVES
4

HEAT
DIRECT
400°F (204°C)

COOKING SURFACE
CAST IRON GRATE

Nothing compares with the decadence of lobster, especially when grilled and stuffed with breadcrumbs. Grilling intensifies the sweetness of the meat and infuses it with a slightly charred flavor.

GRILLED LOBSTER
with buttery herbed breadcrumbs

INGREDIENTS

½ bunch of fresh flat-leaf parsley, chopped

4 sprigs of fresh thyme, leaves only

5 garlic cloves, coarsely chopped

¼ cup unsalted butter, melted

kosher salt and freshly ground black pepper

2 cups panko breadcrumbs

2 whole lobsters, about 2lb (1kg) in total, split lengthwise and cleaned at the fish counter

2 tbsp olive oil

lemon wedges, to serve

METHOD

1 Preheat the grill to 400°F (204°C) using direct heat with a cast iron grate installed. In a food processor, combine parsley, thyme, garlic, and butter, and pulse until a cohesive mixture forms. Season with salt and pepper to taste, then add the breadcrumbs and pulse a couple times just to combine.

2 Drizzle lobster with a little oil, then pack the body cavity with the breadcrumb mixture. Place lobsters on the grate shell side down, close the lid, and grill until breadcrumbs are golden brown, about 12 to 18 minutes, keeping the lobster shells between the fire and the tender meat.

3 Remove lobster from the grill, and serve immediately with lemon wedges to squeeze over top.

TIP

Purchase live lobsters at the fish counter and have the fishmonger split and clean them. Grill the fresh lobsters the same day.

PREP TIME
1 HR

COOK TIME
10-20 MINS

SERVES
4

HEAT
**DIRECT
500°F (260°C)**

COOKING SURFACE
CAST IRON GRATE

Crunchy wontons, sliced tuna, and a smooth salsa featuring
jalapeño and avocado create different textures with every bite.
Searing the tuna locks in flavors from the salsa marinade.

SEARED TUNA
with avocado salsa

INGREDIENTS

1lb (450g) skinless ahi tuna steak,
 cut into 2-in (5-cm) pieces
12 wonton wrappers
vegetable oil
fresh cilantro, to garnish

for the salsa

1 jalapeño pepper
1 ripe avocado
1 cup water
1 tbsp white vinegar
¾ tsp kosher salt
2 tbsp minced fresh cilantro
2 tbsp diced red onion

METHOD

1 Preheat the grill to 500°F (260°C) using direct heat with a cast iron grate
installed. Place jalapeño on the grate, close the lid, and grill until charred,
about 7 to 10 minutes.

2 To make the salsa, in a food processor, combine jalapeño, avocado, water,
vinegar, and salt. Purée for several seconds until jalapeño is finely minced.
Transfer to a medium bowl, add cilantro and onion, and stir to combine.

3 Place tuna in a resealable plastic bag, add enough salsa to coat, and refrigerate
for 1 hour. Cover remaining salsa and refrigerate until ready to use.

4 Brush wonton wrappers with a light coating of oil, place on the grate, close the lid,
and grill until crispy, about 2 to 4 minutes per side, turning as necessary. Once
crisp, arrange on a serving platter.

5 Remove tuna from the marinade, place on the grate, close the lid, and sear for
1 to 2 minutes, flipping once. (The center should be rare.)

6 Remove tuna from the grill, slice thinly, place on wontons, and top with more salsa
and cilantro. Serve immediately.

TIP The salsa in this recipe pairs well with other
varieties of fish, such as salmon, bass, or snapper,
but these should be grilled a little longer so they
aren't rare in the center.

PREP TIME
20 MINS

COOK TIME
50-55 MINS

SERVES
4

HEAT
DIRECT
425ºF (218ºC)

COOKING SURFACE
CAST IRON GRATE
DUTCH OVEN

Sea bass takes on the flavors of miso and the smoking wood when poached on the kamado grill. It's served here as an elegantly composed salad, with hard-boiled eggs and grilled vegetables.

MISO POACHED SEA BASS
with grilled vegetables & Dijon dressing

INGREDIENTS

4 large eggs

3 tbsp white miso paste

4 sea bass fillets, about 6oz (170g) each, skinned and deboned

3 medium red-skinned potatoes

12 fresh green beans

1 red onion

1 medium head of butter lettuce

2 large beefsteak tomatoes, sliced

16 Kalamata olives, pitted

4 tbsp capers

2 tbsp chopped fresh flat-leaf parsley

for the dressing

4 garlic cloves, crushed

2 tsp Dijon mustard

6 tbsp extra virgin olive oil

2 tbsp soy sauce

2 tbsp white miso

3 tbsp rice vinegar

kosher salt and freshly ground black pepper

to smoke

grapevine or apple wood chunks

METHOD

1 Place eggs in a medium saucepan and cover with cold water. Cover the pot with a lid and bring to a boil on the stovetop over high heat. Once boiling, remove the pot from the heat, keep it covered, and let sit for 20 minutes. Drain the water, and set eggs aside to cool. Once cool, peel, halve, and refrigerate until ready to use.

2 To make the dressing, in a small bowl, whisk together garlic, Dijon mustard, oil, soy sauce, miso, and rice vinegar. Season with salt and pepper to taste, and set aside.

3 Preheat the grill to 425°F (218°C) using direct heat with a cast iron grate installed. Add enough water in the Dutch oven to cover bass. (Don't add bass to the water yet.) Place the Dutch oven on the grate, leave the lid off the Dutch oven, and close the grill lid.

4 Once the water starts to simmer, place the wood chunks on the coals. Add miso paste, stirring to dissolve, and then add fish fillets. Leave the lid off the Dutch oven, close the grill lid, and cook until cooked through, about 10 minutes per inch of thickness. Remove from the water and set aside.

5 Place potatoes, green beans, and onion on the grate around the Dutch oven. Close the lid and grill until charred, about 7 to 10 minutes. Remove the vegetables from the grill, and chop potatoes and onion. Place the vegetables in a medium bowl, add the dressing, and stir to coat.

6 Line a serving platter with the large outer lettuce leaves. Chop the remainder and arrange on the platter. Place tomato slices on one end of the platter, followed by the grilled vegetables. (Don't throw out the dressing from the bowl.) Place fish in the center of the platter. Garnish with sliced hard-boiled eggs, olives, and capers. Sprinkle parsley over top and drizzle the remaining dressing before serving.

Grilled on a cedar wood plank, this lime-glazed salmon has a burnished exterior and a deliciously buttery texture. Brining ensures that the fish is moist and flavorful.

CEDAR-PLANK SALMON
with ginger lime sauce

INGREDIENTS

1½lb (680g) skinless salmon, cut from the thickest part of the fish

for the brine

²/₃ cup kosher salt

²/₃ cup packed light brown sugar

4 tbsp pickling spice

8 cups hot water

for the sauce

2 limes

2 garlic cloves, minced

1 tbsp extra virgin olive oil

1 tbsp honey

1 tbsp soy sauce

1 tsp chopped fresh mint leaves, plus more to garnish

1-in (2.5-cm) piece ginger, peeled and grated

kosher salt and freshly ground black pepper

METHOD

1 Place a 4 x 9in (10 x 23cm) cedar wood plank in a baking dish, cover with cold water, and place heavy cans or stones on the plank to keep it submerged. Soak for 1 to 2 hours.

2 To make the brine, in a large bowl, whisk together salt, brown sugar, pickling spice, and water until salt and sugar have dissolved. Add ice cubes a few at a time until the liquid is no longer hot. Place the salmon in a large resealable plastic bag and add brine to fully cover. (Any extra brine can be refrigerated and saved for a later use.) Refrigerate for 1 hour.

3 To make the sauce, grate the zest from 1 lime into a small bowl. Squeeze the juice of both limes and add to the bowl, then whisk in garlic, oil, honey, soy sauce, mint, and ginger. Taste and season with salt and pepper.

4 Preheat the grill to 400°F (204°C) using direct heat with a standard grate installed. Remove the cedar plank from the water and pat dry with paper towels. Place the plank on the grate until it starts to crackle and some coloring and charring appear, about 3 minutes, then turn the plank over.

5 Remove salmon from the brine and place it on the hot side of the plank. Generously brush salmon with lime sauce, close the lid, and grill until the fish is just cooked through and slightly flaky but still moist, about 12 to 15 minutes.

6 Remove salmon from the grill, lightly brush with some of the remaining sauce, and garnish with mint leaves. Serve immediately.

SIDES

PREP TIME
20 MINS

COOK TIME
20-30 MINS

SERVES
6

HEAT
DIRECT
400°F (204°C)

COOKING SURFACE
CAST IRON GRATE

This colorful salad is bursting with the summery flavors of grilled vegetables and fresh herbs. Briefly marinating the vegetables in the balsamic dressing brings out more flavor.

GRILLED VEGETABLE & COUSCOUS SALAD

INGREDIENTS

1 small zucchini, halved

1 small yellow squash, halved

½ red onion

6 sun-dried tomatoes

1 tbsp olive oil

2 cups uncooked Israeli couscous

4 cups vegetable stock, heated

4 basil leaves, stacked, rolled, and cut crosswise into thin strips, plus more to garnish

2 tbsp coarsely chopped fresh flat-leaf parsley, plus more to garnish

for the marinade

¼ cup balsamic vinegar

½ tsp Dijon mustard

1 garlic clove, coarsely chopped

½ cup olive oil

kosher salt and freshly ground black pepper

METHOD

1 To make the marinade, in a small bowl, whisk together vinegar, mustard, and garlic. Slowly add oil, whisking until combined. Season with salt and pepper to taste.

2 Place zucchini, yellow squash, onion, and sun-dried tomatoes in a shallow dish. Pour half the marinade over the vegetables, toss to coat, and let sit at room temperature for 15 minutes. Cover the remaining marinade and set aside.

3 Preheat the grill to 400°F (204°C) with a cast iron grate installed and a Dutch oven on the grate. Remove the vegetables from the marinade and place on the grate around the Dutch oven. Close the lid and grill until beginning to soften and char, about 7 to 10 minutes. Transfer the vegetables to a cutting board and cut into bite-sized pieces. Set aside.

4 In the hot Dutch oven, heat oil until shimmering. Add couscous, and toast until lightly golden brown, about 2 minutes. Add vegetable stock until couscous is just covered (add hot water if more liquid is needed to cover), close the grill lid, and bring to a boil. Cook until firm to the bite, about 7 to 10 minutes, and drain well.

5 Spoon the couscous into a large serving bowl and add the grilled vegetables, basil, and parsley. Drizzle the reserved marinade over top, and toss well to coat. Serve at room temperature with more basil and parsley to garnish.

PREP TIME **20 MINS**	COOK TIME **25-30 MINS**	SERVES **8**	HEAT **DIRECT 400°F (204°C)**	COOKING SURFACE **CAST IRON GRATE DUTCH OVEN**

Spicy, savory Mexican rice is the perfect accompaniment to tacos, smoked meat, or any kind of steak. This homemade version has robust flavor and more vegetables than a typical Tex-Mex dish.

ARROZ A LA MEXICANA
(MEXICAN RICE)

INGREDIENTS

2 small white onions, peeled and halved

2 poblano peppers, left whole

2 carrots, peeled

¼ cup vegetable oil

3 garlic cloves, minced

2 cups uncooked white rice

4 cups chicken stock

¼ cup tomato paste

1½ tbsp ground cumin

1 bunch of fresh cilantro, chopped

METHOD

1 Preheat the grill to 400°F (204°C) using direct heat with a cast iron grate installed and a Dutch oven on the grate. Place onions, peppers, and carrots on the grate around the Dutch oven, close the lid, and grill until beginning to soften and char, about 7 to 10 minutes. Remove the vegetables from the grill, chop onions and peppers, and dice carrots into small cubes.

2 In the hot Dutch oven, heat oil until shimmering. Add carrots, and cook for 2 minutes, stirring occasionally. Stir in onions and garlic, and cook for 1 minute, stirring occasionally. Add rice, stock, tomato paste, and cumin. Bring to a boil, stirring once or twice. Cover the Dutch oven with its lid and close the grill lid. Cook until rice is tender and liquid is absorbed, about 15 minutes.

3 Remove the Dutch oven from the grill, stir peppers and cilantro into the rice, and fluff the rice with a fork. Serve immediately.

 TIP
Rice won't stick to a well-seasoned Dutch oven. To season, scrub with hot soapy water and dry well. Spread vegetable oil inside, place upside down in an oven at 375°F (191°C), and bake for 1 hour. Let cool.

PREP TIME
20 MINS

COOK TIME
20-40 MINS

SERVES
6

HEAT
DIRECT
350ºF (177ºC)

COOKING SURFACE
CAST IRON GRATE
DUTCH OVEN

This simple side comes together quickly, with grilled vegetables and aromatics infusing black beans with flavor. Serve alongside tacos, add to a burrito bowl, or enjoy the beans on their own.

DUTCH OVEN BLACK BEANS

INGREDIENTS

1 medium yellow onion, peeled and halved

1 green bell pepper, left whole

2 x 15oz (425g) cans black beans with liquid or 3 cups cooked black beans

2 garlic cloves, minced

1 tsp ground cumin

½ tsp dried oregano

½ tsp kosher salt

1 tsp red wine vinegar

1 bunch of fresh cilantro, chopped

METHOD

1 Preheat the grill to 350°F (177°C) using direct heat with a cast iron grate installed and a Dutch oven on the grate. Arrange onions and pepper on the grate around the Dutch oven, close the grill lid, and grill until beginning to soften and char, about 5 to 7 minutes. Transfer the vegetables to a cutting board and chop.

2 Add ⅛ cup bean liquid to the Dutch oven. Add onion, pepper, and garlic, close the grill lid, and sauté until soft, about 2 minutes. Add beans with the remaining liquid. Stir in cumin, oregano, and salt. Cover the Dutch oven with its lid and close the grill lid. Simmer for 15 to 30 minutes.

3 Remove the Dutch oven from the grill and stir in the vinegar and cilantro, reserving a bit to sprinkle over top. Serve immediately.

TIP

To cook dried black beans , place beans in a pot and add water to cover by about 3 inches (8 cm). Cover and bring to a boil, then remove the lid and simmer until beans are tender, about 1 to 2 hours.

PREP TIME
20 MINS

COOK TIME
30-35 MINS

SERVES
6

HEAT
**INDIRECT
350ºF (177ºC)**

COOKING SURFACE
**STANDARD GRATE
DUTCH OVEN**

The flavor of this creamy Italian dish depends on the quality of your chicken stock, so use the best you can find. Onion and garlic lend a savory note, and tomatoes give the dish a pop of red.

CHEESY TOMATO RISOTTO

INGREDIENTS

1 tbsp unsalted butter

½ red onion, chopped

3 garlic cloves, minced

¾ cup Arborio rice

3 cups chicken stock, warmed, plus more as needed

2 medium Roma tomatoes, diced small

2oz (55g) freshly shredded Parmesan cheese

2 scallions, thinly sliced

1 tbsp chopped fresh flat-leaf parsley

METHOD

1 Preheat the grill to 350ºF (177°C) using indirect heat with a standard grate installed and a Dutch oven on the grate. In the hot Dutch oven, melt butter. Add onion and garlic, close the grill lid, and cook until barely beginning to soften, about 2 minutes. Add rice, stir, and close the grill lid. Cook until rice is coated with butter and slightly toasted, about 2 to 3 minutes.

2 Add warm stock to the rice 1 cup at a time, stirring often. Add more stock only after the liquid from the previous addition is absorbed. (This will take about 10 minutes each time you add the liquid.) Add tomatoes and cheese, and stir until cheese melts. Add scallions and parsley, and stir until just combined. Remove the Dutch oven from the grill and serve immediately.

TIP For a more uniform texture, grate the tomatoes instead of dicing them. Cut them in half, hold the skin against your hand, and gently slide the fleshy part across a box grater.

PREP TIME
20 MINS

COOK TIME
1 HR

SERVES
10

HEAT
**INDIRECT
400°F (204°C)**

COOKING SURFACE
**STANDARD GRATE
BAKING DISH**

Aromatic sage and a hint of nutmeg season these creamy, tender potatoes, which are layered with Asiago cheese and topped with crunchy breadcrumbs for a hearty and comforting dish.

ASIAGO & SAGE SCALLOPED POTATOES

INGREDIENTS

2 tbsp unsalted butter

2 medium yellow onions, thinly sliced

½ tsp finely chopped garlic

2 bay leaves

¼ tsp grated fresh nutmeg

1 tbsp kosher salt

¾ tsp ground black pepper

1¼ cups heavy cream

½ cup whole milk

2 tbsp finely chopped fresh sage

2½lb (1.1kg) Idaho potatoes, peeled and thinly sliced

for the topping

1 cup freshly grated Asiago cheese, about 3oz (85g) in total

1 cup plain breadcrumbs

2 tbsp extra virgin olive oil

¼ tsp kosher salt

¼ tsp ground black pepper

1½ tsp finely chopped fresh sage

METHOD

1 Preheat the grill to 400°F (204°C) using indirect heat with a standard grate installed. Place a large heavy-bottomed saucepan on the grate and melt butter. Add onions, close the lid, and grill until golden brown, about 8 minutes, stirring often.

2 Add garlic, bay leaves, nutmeg, salt, and pepper, and cook for 30 seconds. Add heavy cream and milk, and bring to a boil. Remove from the heat, cover, and let sit for 5 minutes. Remove bay leaves and stir in sage.

3 To make the topping, in a medium bowl, toss cheese with breadcrumbs, olive oil, salt, pepper, and sage.

4 In a large bowl, gently toss potatoes with the onion mixture. Spread half the potatoes and liquid in a 2-quart (2-liter) grill-safe baking dish and sprinkle ⅔ cup of the cheese and breadcrumb mixture over top. Add the remaining potatoes to the dish, pressing firmly to pack them down. Spoon any remaining liquid over the potatoes and cover with the remaining breadcrumbs.

5 Place the dish on the grate, close the grill lid, and cook until potatoes are fork tender and the top is golden brown, about 1 hour. (If the top browns too quickly, loosely cover the dish with aluminum foil). Remove potatoes from the grill and serve hot.

PREP TIME
20 MINS

COOK TIME
30 MINS

SERVES
8

HEAT
INDIRECT
350°F (177°C)

COOKING SURFACE
STANDARD GRATE
CAST IRON SKILLET

This savory pudding is somewhere between a soufflé and a spoon bread. Studded with grilled corn and a poblano pepper, it has a hearty texture and smoky flavor with just a hint of sweetness.

CORN & POBLANO PUDDING

INGREDIENTS

vegetable oil, for greasing

4 ears of sweet corn, shucked

1 poblano pepper, left whole

4 large eggs

1 cup whole milk

½ tsp kosher salt

¼ tsp ground nutmeg

¼ tsp ground cayenne pepper

2oz (55g) shredded Cheddar cheese

METHOD

1 Preheat the grill to 350°F (177°C) using indirect heat with a standard grate installed. Grease a cast iron skillet with oil.

2 Place corn and pepper on the grate, positioning them around the edges, close the lid, and grill until beginning to soften and char, about 10 minutes. Transfer the vegetables to a cutting board, cut the kernels from the cobs, and seed and dice the pepper.

3 In a large bowl, whisk together eggs, milk, salt, nutmeg, cayenne, and cheese until well combined. Stir in corn kernels and pepper. Pour the mixture into the greased dish and place on the grate. Close the lid and bake until a knife inserted halfway between the center and the outer edge comes out clean, about 20 minutes. Remove the pudding from the grill and serve warm or at room temperature.

TIP
To make individual servings, prepare the pudding in a 12-hole muffin pan. Grease the pan with oil and cook on the grill for 10 minutes.

PREP TIME **20 MINS**	COOK TIME **35–40 MINS**	SERVES **16**	HEAT **INDIRECT 400°F (204°C)**	COOKING SURFACE **CAST IRON GRATE DUTCH OVEN**

This hearty side dish begins by rendering bacon, giving the beans a smoky, meaty character that's complemented by the Asian-inspired flavors of soy sauce, ginger, and five-spice powder.

DUTCH OVEN BAKED BEANS

INGREDIENTS

6 scallions, plus more to garnish

1lb (450g) bacon, diced

3 garlic cloves

4 x 15oz (420g) cans Great Northern beans

2 tbsp Chinese five-spice powder

½ cup chopped fresh cilantro

2 tbsp black bean garlic sauce

2 tsp ground ginger

3 tbsp soy sauce

1 cup sweet chili sauce

METHOD

1 Preheat the grill to 400°F (204°C) using indirect heat with a cast iron grate installed and a Dutch oven on the grate. Place scallions on the grate around the Dutch oven, close the grill lid, and grill until beginning to char, about 2 minutes. Chop scallions and set aside.

2 Place bacon in the Dutch oven, close the grill lid, and cook until crisp, about 15 to 20 minutes, stirring occasionally. Use a slotted spoon to remove bacon from the Dutch oven and set aside.

3 Drain all but 2 tbsp bacon fat from the Dutch oven. Add scallions and garlic, close the grill lid, and cook until just fragrant, about 1 minute. Add beans, five-spice powder, cilantro, garlic sauce, ginger, soy sauce, and chili sauce, and stir to combine. Place the lid on the Dutch oven, close the grill lid, and cook beans until heated through, about 15 minutes.

4 Remove the Dutch oven from the grill, and stir bacon into the baked beans. Garnish with sliced scallions, and serve immediately.

 Use any variety of white bean for this dish, such as navy beans or cannellini beans. These mild, hearty beans will retain their shape and soak up the savory flavors of the dish.

PREP TIME **20 MINS**	COOK TIME **20 MINS**	SERVES **8**	HEAT **INDIRECT 425°F (218°C)**	COOKING SURFACE **STANDARD GRATE WOOD PLANK**

Plump tomatoes are stuffed with breadcrumbs and cheese, then grilled on a cedar plank, which imparts a subtle woodsy flavor and prevents the tomatoes from drying out while they roast.

WOOD-PLANK STUFFED TOMATOES

INGREDIENTS

4 beefsteak tomatoes

1 cup chopped fresh flat-leaf parsley

¾ cup Italian-style breadcrumbs

1 cup grated provolone

¼ tsp ground black pepper

1 tsp unsalted butter, softened

2 tbsp extra virgin olive oil

METHOD

1 Place a 4 x 9in (10 x 23cm) wood plank in a baking dish, cover with cold water, and place heavy cans or stones on the plank to keep it submerged. Soak for 1 to 2 hours.

2 Preheat the grill to 425°F (218°C) using indirect heat with a standard grate installed. Place the wood plank on the grate.

3 Cut tomatoes in half horizontally and hollow out the insides, discarding the seeds and reserving the pulp. Chop the reserved pulp and place in a medium bowl. Add parsley, breadcrumbs, provolone, and pepper, and mix gently to combine. Fill each tomato half with the breadcrumb mixture and top with a drizzle of oil.

4 Flip the plank over, spread butter on the hot side, and arrange tomatoes cut side up on the plank. Place the plank on the grate, close the lid, and cook until the tops are browned and the tomatoes are soft, about 20 minutes. Remove tomatoes from the grill and serve immediately.

 TIP Choose natural and untreated Western red cedar or alder wood for making this dish. Both offer a light, sweet flavor that's not overpowering.

PREP TIME
1-2 HOUR

COOK TIME
40-50 MINS

SERVES
16

HEAT
DIRECT
400°F (204°C)

COOKING SURFACE
STANDARD GRATE
CAST IRON SKILLET
WOOD PLANK

These are the ultimate mashed potatoes. Loaded with cheese, sour cream, and salty bits of bacon, they're piled on a cedar plank and grilled for an incomparable smoky flavor and rustic presentation.

WOOD-PLANK LOADED MASHED POTATOES

INGREDIENTS

1lb (450g) red potatoes

1lb (450g) Yukon Gold potatoes

1 tbsp kosher salt, plus 1 tsp

2 strips bacon, diced

2 tbsp unsalted butter

¼ cup sour cream

¼ cup heavy cream

4oz (113g) shredded Cheddar cheese, plus more for topping

4 scallions, thinly sliced, plus more for topping

freshly ground black pepper

METHOD

1 Place a 4 x 9in (10 x 23cm) cedar wood plank in a baking dish, cover with cold water, and place heavy cans or stones on the plank to keep it submerged. Soak for 1 to 2 hours.

2 Place red potatoes and Yukon Gold potatoes in a large stockpot and add cold water to cover by several inches. Place the pot on the stovetop over high heat, add 1 tsp salt, and bring to a boil. Reduce to a simmer, cover, and cook until potatoes are fork tender, about 25 minutes. Drain potatoes, reserving 1 cup cooking water.

3 Preheat the grill to 350°F (177°C) using direct heat with a standard grate installed and a cast iron skillet on the grate. Add bacon to the hot skillet, and cook until bacon is crisp and the fat has rendered, about 10 to 15 minutes, stirring occasionally. Transfer the cooked bacon pieces to a plate lined with a paper towel.

4 In a large bowl, combine potatoes, butter, sour cream, heavy cream, Cheddar cheese, scallions, bacon, and 1 tbsp salt. Mash with a potato masher until potatoes have broken down and cheese and sour cream are fully incorporated. If potatoes are too stiff, add some of the reserved cooking water.

5 Place the soaked plank on the grate and allow it to heat for 2 to 5 minutes, then flip it over. Scoop the mashed potatoes onto the heated side of the plank. Top the potatoes with a little Cheddar cheese, close the lid, and cook until cheese has melted and potatoes have browned slightly, about 7 to 10 minutes. Remove potatoes from the grill, sprinkle with scallions, and serve immediately.

PREP TIME
20 MINS

COOK TIME
40-45 MINS

SERVES
9

HEAT
INDIRECT
400°F (204°C)

COOKING SURFACE
STANDARD GRATE
CAST IRON SKILLET
WOOD PLANK

Jerk seasoning—with spices that run the gamut from salty and sweet to mildly hot and en fuego—brings a little of the Caribbean to these colorful stuffed bell peppers.

CARIBBEAN STUFFED PEPPERS

INGREDIENTS

3 tbsp olive oil

2lb (1kg) ground sausage meat

1 red onion, diced

5 garlic cloves, minced

4½ tbsp jerk seasoning

½ cup cooked brown rice

3 cups chicken stock

3 tomatoes, skins and stems removed, diced

1 fresh habanero pepper

6 sprigs of fresh thyme

3 bay leaves

¼-inch (.5-cm) piece fresh ginger, minced

2 x 15oz (425g) cans black beans, drained and rinsed

2 bunches of fresh cilantro, chopped

4 scallions, thinly sliced

juice of 3 limes

9 bell peppers, any color, tops and ribs removed and seeded

3oz (85g) queso fresco, crumbled

METHOD

1 Place two 4 x 9in (10 x 23cm) wood planks in a baking dish, cover with cold water, and place heavy cans or stones on the planks to keep them submerged. Soak for 1 to 2 hours.

2 Preheat the grill to 400°F (204°C) using indirect heat with a standard grate installed and a cast iron skillet on the grate. In the hot skillet, heat oil until shimmering. Add sausage, onion, and garlic, close the lid, and cook until the meat begins to brown, about 3 to 4 minutes. Add jerk seasoning, stir, and close the lid. Cook until the meat is completely cooked, about 3 to 4 minutes more.

3 Add rice, stock, tomatoes, habanero, thyme, bay leaves, and ginger to the sausage mixture, and stir gently. Close the lid and cook until heated through, about 4 minutes. Remove the skillet from the heat and set aside to cool for 10 minutes. Place the wood planks on the grate to heat while the filling cools. (Be sure to have enough space on the planks to hold all the peppers.)

4 Once the filling has cooled, discard habanero, thyme sprigs, and bay leaves. Gently stir in beans, cilantro, scallions, and lime juice. Place peppers on a baking sheet (to make them easier to carry to the grill) and fill with the rice mixture until all the filling is used up. (If peppers won't sit upright, cut a thin slice off the bottom, taking care not to create a hole.)

5 Transfer peppers to the hot wood planks, close the lid, and grill until the ingredients are fully cooked and heated through, about 30 minutes.

6 Remove stuffed peppers from the grill, sprinkle with cheese, and serve immediately.

PREP TIME **20 MINS**	COOK TIME **7-10 MINS**	SERVES **8**	HEAT **DIRECT** **425°F (218°C)**	COOKING SURFACE **CAST IRON GRATE**

No need for tortilla chips—this salsa is so good, you might want to eat it straight from the bowl. Savory rather than spicy, it features grilled corn and avocado, fresh tomatoes, and blue cheese.

CORN & TOMATO SALSA
with blue cheese & basil

INGREDIENTS

6 ears of corn, shucked

1 lime, halved

1 avocado, halved

1lb (450g) grape tomatoes, quartered

½ tsp kosher salt, plus more as needed

½ tsp ground black pepper, plus more as needed

2 tsp olive oil

4oz (110g) blue cheese, crumbled

10 fresh basil leaves, sliced

METHOD

1 Preheat the grill to 425°F (218°C) using direct heat with a cast iron grate installed. Place corn, avocado, and lime on the grate, close the lid, and grill until beginning to soften and char, about 7 to 10 minutes. Transfer the corn, avocado, and lime to a cutting board. Cut the kernels from the corn and dice the avocado.

2 In a large bowl, gently combine corn, tomatoes, avocado, salt, and pepper. Squeeze the grilled lime over top, drizzle with olive oil, and toss to coat.

3 Top the corn mixture with blue cheese and basil, and toss one final time. Season with salt and pepper to taste. Serve immediately.

 You can add other vegetables to this salsa, including onion, zucchini, and jicama, which is a Mexican turnip. Grill these vegetables along with the corn and avocado.

PREP TIME
20 MINS

COOK TIME
35–40 MINS

SERVES
4

HEAT
**INDIRECT
350°F (177°C)**

COOKING SURFACE
**CAST IRON GRATE
CAST IRON SKILLET**

This salty, hearty hash is a welcome addition to any breakfast table. Full of smoky flavor from the bacon and chorizo, it's delicious alongside a cheesy omelette or topped with a poached egg.

CORN, BACON & CHORIZO HASH

INGREDIENTS

4 ears of corn, shucked

2 Fresno peppers

1lb (450g) new potatoes, halved if large

8oz (225g) chorizo sausage, casings removed

8oz (225g) thick-cut bacon, diced

2 shallots, finely diced

kosher salt and freshly ground black pepper

METHOD

1 Preheat the grill to 350°F (117°C) using indirect heat with a cast iron grate installed and a cast iron skillet on the grate. Place corn, peppers, and potatoes on the grate around the skillet, close the grill lid, and grill until beginning to soften and char, about 6 to 10 minutes. (Peppers and corn cook more quickly than the potatoes.) Remove the vegetables from the grill. Cut the kernels from the cobs, seed and dice the peppers, and dice the potatoes. Set aside.

2 In the hot skillet, cook chorizo for 10 minutes, stirring once or twice. Transfer the cooked chorizo to a platter and set aside. Return the skillet to the grill, add bacon, close the grill lid, and cook until crisp and the fat has rendered, about 10 minutes. Drain the bacon grease, reserving 1 tbsp in the skillet along with the cooked bacon, and return the skillet to the grill.

3 Add shallots to the skillet, close the grill lid, and sauté until soft and translucent, about 2 minutes. Add corn kernels, potatoes, and chorizo, close the grill lid, and sauté for 5 to 7 minutes more. Add half the diced peppers and season with salt and pepper. Taste to check the spice level before adding the remaining diced peppers. Stir and cook for 1 minute more. Remove the hash from the grill and serve immediately.

TIP Instead of a Fresno pepper, you could use a jalapeño pepper or a chipotle pepper for a smoky flavor or a serrano pepper for more heat.

PREP TIME **20 MINS**	COOK TIME **15-20 MINS**	SERVES **12**	HEAT **DIRECT** **400°F (204°C)**	COOKING SURFACE **CAST IRON GRATE**

Sweet, spicy, and salty, these snackable sweet potatoes will satisfy all your taste buds. Coating them with maple syrup and seasonings before grilling gives them a flavorful, caramelized exterior.

GRILLED SWEET POTATOES
with maple & thyme

INGREDIENTS

5 tbsp olive oil

5 tbsp pure maple syrup

3 tbsp kosher salt

6 garlic cloves, minced, plus more to serve

2 tsp finely chopped fresh thyme leaves

¼ tsp crushed red pepper flakes

6 large sweet potatoes, about 3lb (1.4kg) in total, peeled and cut into thick wedges

2 tbsp finely chopped fresh flat-leaf parsley

METHOD

1 Preheat the grill to 400°F (204°C) using direct heat with a cast iron grate installed.

2 In a large bowl, whisk together oil, syrup, salt, garlic, thyme, and red pepper flakes. Add potatoes and toss to coat. Season with more salt (if desired).

3 Place wedges on the grate, being sure to shake off excess liquid, close the lid, and grill until lightly golden brown and just cooked through, about 15 to 20 minutes, turning often.

4 Transfer to a serving bowl and immediately toss with parsley and more minced garlic (if desired). Season with salt to taste.

 TIP Leave the skins on the sweet potatoes for an even crunchier texture. Plus, the skins provide nutrients that complement what the flesh offers.

PREP TIME
20 MINS

COOK TIME
7-10 MINS

SERVES
10

HEAT
DIRECT
425ºF (218ºC)

COOKING SURFACE
CAST IRON GRATE

Forget store-bought potato salad. Grilled potatoes deliver the flavor of campfire cooking, and peppers, red onion, and celery add crunch and color to this creamy salad.

CAMPFIRE POTATO SALAD

INGREDIENTS

2lb (1kg) new potatoes, unpeeled
1 green bell pepper, left whole
1 red bell pepper, left whole
½ red onion
¼ cup mayonnaise
¼ cup sour cream
1 tbsp Dijon mustard
¾ tsp garlic, minced
1 tbsp kosher salt
¼ tsp ground black pepper
1 tbsp chopped fresh dill
2 celery stalks, diced

METHOD

1 Preheat the grill to 425°F (218°C) using direct heat with a cast iron grate installed. Place potatoes, peppers, and onion on the grate, close the lid, and grill until beginning to soften and char, about 7 to 10 minutes, turning once or twice.

2 Remove the vegetables from the grill and let cool slightly. Cut the potatoes into quarters and dice the peppers and onion.

3 In a large bowl, combine mayonnaise, sour cream, mustard, garlic, salt, pepper, and dill. Add potatoes, peppers, onions, and celery to the mayonnaise mixture, and gently combine until the vegetables are evenly coated with the dressing. Taste and adjust the seasoning as needed. Serve warm.

TIP

Leave the potatoes on the grate (but remove the peppers and onions) and grill them a little longer for a softer texture—and softer bite.

PREP TIME
20 MINS

COOK TIME
30 MINS

SERVES
20

HEAT
**INDIRECT
425°F (218°C)**

COOKING SURFACE
**STANDARD GRATE
CAST IRON SKILLET**

Bold flavors elevate the humble roasted potatoes in this simple side. Sharp vinegar and salty queso fresco mingle with pungent garlic and charred poblanos, creating an addictive, crave-worthy dish.

ROASTED POTATOES
with poblanos & queso fresco

INGREDIENTS

2lb (1kg) fingerling potatoes, halved

1 tbsp chopped fresh cilantro

1 tbsp chopped fresh basil

1 tbsp chopped scallions, plus more to garnish

3 poblano peppers, diced

½ cup olive oil

½ cup white vinegar

3 garlic cloves, minced

kosher salt and freshly ground black pepper

1 cup crumbled queso fresco

METHOD

1 Preheat the grill to 425°F (218°C) using indirect heat with a standard grate installed. In a Dutch oven or a disposable aluminum baking dish, combine potatoes, cilantro, basil, scallions, peppers, oil, vinegar, and garlic. Toss well to ensure potatoes are coated in oil and seasonings. Place the Dutch oven on the grate and cook until potatoes are fork tender, about 30 minutes.

2 Remove the Dutch oven from the grill, season with salt and pepper to taste, and top with the queso fresco and more sliced scallions. Serve immediately.

TIP

Any variety of potato can be used, but multi-colored fingerlings make for an impressive presentation. Cut them into chunks of similar size for even cooking.

PREP TIME
30 MINS

COOK TIME
60-70 MINS

SERVES
8

HEAT
**INDIRECT
350ºF (177ºC)**

COOKING SURFACE
**CAST IRON GRATE
CAST IRON SKILLET**

Grilled potatoes have more flavor and a better texture than the boiled potatoes that are traditionally used. Bacon adds a smoky richness that complements the tangy bite of vinegar and mustard.

GERMAN POTATO SALAD

INGREDIENTS

2lb (1kg) Yukon Gold potatoes, unpeeled and cut into rounds or bite-sized pieces

½lb (225g) thick-cut bacon

¾ cup finely chopped yellow onion

⅓ cup white vinegar

¼ cup sugar

1 tbsp Dijon mustard

1 tsp kosher salt

2 tbsp minced chives, to garnish

METHOD

1 Preheat the grill to 350ºF (177ºC) using indirect heat with a cast iron grate installed and a cast iron skillet on the grate. Place potatoes on the grate around the skillet, close the lid, and roast until fork tender, about 45 minutes. Remove potatoes from the grill and set aside.

2 Add bacon to the hot skillet, close the lid, and cook until crisp, about 10 to 15 minutes. Once crisp, transfer to a plate lined with a paper towel and crumble into small pieces. Pour off the rendered fat, reserving 4 tbsp in the skillet.

3 Add onion to the skillet, close the lid, and cook until translucent and beginning to brown, about 4 to 5 minutes. Whisk in vinegar, sugar, mustard, and salt, and stir until thick and bubbly, about 2 to 3 minutes. Add the cooked potatoes, and toss to coat.

4 Remove the skillet from the grill, top with crumbled bacon, and garnish with chives. Serve warm.

TIP Try mixing in the bacon and chives rather than sprinkling them on top of the potato salad, and use red potatoes if you prefer them to Yukon Gold.

PREP TIME
20 MINS

COOK TIME
25-30 MINS

SERVES
6

HEAT
DIRECT
400°F (204°C)

COOKING SURFACE
CAST IRON GRATE
CAST IRON SKILLET

Buckwheat soba noodles have a slightly nutty taste that pairs well with the spicy peanut sauce and grilled vegetables in this creamy side. Cabbage, carrot, and peppers add a colorful crunch.

SOBA NOODLE BOWL
with peanut sauce

INGREDIENTS

12oz (28g) soba noodles
4 scallions
2 red bell peppers, left whole
1 carrot, peeled
½ head of napa cabbage
¼ cup chopped hazelnuts
chopped fresh cilantro, to garnish

for the sauce

½ cup peanut butter
¼ cup soy sauce
⅓ cup warm water
2 tbsp ground ginger
1 garlic clove
2 tbsp white wine vinegar
1½ tsp honey
1 tsp crushed red pepper flakes

METHOD

1 To make the sauce, combine all the sauce ingredients in a blender and purée until smooth. Set aside. (Sauce can be made in advance. Refrigerate in an airtight container and use within 1 week.)

2 Cook the pasta according to the package directions until cooked but still firm to the bite. Drain and rinse well under cold water. Set aside.

3 Preheat the grill to 400°F (204°C) using direct heat with a cast iron grate installed and a cast iron skillet on the grate. Place scallions, peppers, carrot, and napa cabbage around the skillet, close the lid, and grill until beginning to soften and char, about 7 to 10 minutes. Slice peppers and carrots thinly, and shred cabbage.

4 Add the vegetables and noodles to the hot skillet, and stir to combine. Add the sauce, and stir until well incorporated and heated through, about 3 to 4 minutes.

5 Remove the skillet from the grill and top noodles with hazelnuts and cilantro. Serve immediately.

PREP TIME
20 MINS

COOK TIME
30–35 MINS

SERVES
6

HEAT
DIRECT
425°F (218°C)

COOKING SURFACE
CAST IRON GRATE
DUTCH OVEN

This dish is reminiscent of ratatouille but forgoes the traditional tomatoes, letting the more subtle flavors of squash and eggplant shine. Garlic, oregano, and lemon lend fragrance and flavor.

SUMMER SQUASH & EGGPLANT
stewed in white wine

INGREDIENTS

1 medium yellow squash

2 medium zucchini

¼ cup olive oil

2 medium yellow onions, sliced into half moons

1 medium eggplant, peeled and cut into cubes

2 garlic cloves, minced

½ tsp dried oregano

2 cups dry white wine, such as Chardonnay

4 tbsp unsalted butter

kosher salt and freshly ground black pepper

lemon slices, to serve (optional)

METHOD

1 Preheat the grill to 425°F (218°C) using direct heat with a cast iron grate installed and a Dutch oven on the grate. Place squash and zucchini on the grate around the Dutch oven, close the lid, and grill until beginning to soften and char, about 5 to 7 minutes. Remove vegetables from the grill and slice into rounds.

2 In the hot Dutch oven, heat oil until shimmering. Add onions, and sauté until translucent, about 7 to 8 minutes. Add squash, zucchini, eggplant, garlic, and oregano. Close the lid and sauté until vegetables begin to soften, about 15 minutes. Add white wine, close the grill lid, and simmer until the vegetables have begun to soften and the liquid has reduced by half, about 5 minutes.

3 Remove the Dutch oven from the grill and add the butter, stirring until melted. Season well with salt and pepper and a squeeze of lemon. Serve hot with lemon slices (if using).

TIP

In cooler months when summer squash is out of season, you can make this dish with winter squash instead. Use butternut, pumpkin, or spaghetti squash—or a combination of all three.

PREP TIME
20 MINS

COOK TIME
4-6 MINS

SERVES
6

HEAT
**DIRECT
500°F (260°C)**

COOKING SURFACE
CAST IRON GRATE

Grilling fruit brings out deeper, richer flavors. This salad pairs sweet grilled watermelon with a tzatziki sauce made with yogurt, cucumbers, and mint for a fresh, tangy twist on the Greek classic.

GRILLED WATERMELON SALAD

INGREDIENTS

4 medium cucumbers, about 1lb (450g) in total, divided

3lb (1.4kg) watermelon, rind removed and cut into thick slices

3 garlic cloves, peeled

1½ cups plain Greek yogurt

⅔ cup chopped mint, divided

¾ tsp kosher salt

2 tbsp fresh lime juice

flaky sea salt, to serve

METHOD

1 Preheat the grill to 500°F (260°C) using direct heat with a cast iron grate installed. Peel 2 cucumbers and halve them lengthwise. Place the halved cucumbers and watermelon slices on the grate, close the lid, and grill until grill marks form, about 2 to 3 minutes per side.

2 Using a chef's knife, finely chop garlic and sprinkle with a pinch of salt. Using the flat of the blade, crush the chopped garlic, scrape into a pile, and crush again, repeating until a paste forms. Transfer to a medium bowl.

3 To make the tzatziki sauce, peel the remaining 2 cucumbers, halve lengthwise, and seed. Coarsely grate into the bowl with the garlic paste. Stir in yogurt, ⅓ cup mint, and salt.

4 Cut the watermelon into bite-sized pieces, and cut the grilled cucumber crosswise into ⅓-in (.75-cm) slices. Place cucumber and watermelon in a large bowl, toss with lime juice and the remaining ⅓ cup mint, and sprinkle with sea salt. Spoon the tzatziki sauce over top to serve.

PREP TIME
20 MINS

COOK TIME
20-30 MINS

SERVES
4-6

HEAT
DIRECT
425ºF (218ºC)

COOKING SURFACE
CAST IRON GRATE
CAST IRON SKILLET

This version of paneer vindaloo is richly aromatic and flavorful. Grilled chunks of paneer—the fresh Indian cheese—are coated in a warmly spiced, tomato-based curry sauce and served with naan.

GRILLED PANEER
with vindaloo curry

INGREDIENTS

4 tbsp unsalted butter
1 medium white onion, diced
3 tbsp chopped fresh ginger
1 jalapeño pepper, diced
1 tbsp vindaloo curry powder
1 tsp kosher salt, divided
28oz (800g) can whole peeled
  tomatoes, preferably fire roasted
½ tsp ground cinnamon
2 tbsp crushed lime leaves
3 tbsp honey
½ cup heavy cream
1lb (450g) paneer cheese,
  thickly sliced
8oz (225g) arugula
¼ cup chopped fresh cilantro
naan bread, to serve (optional)

METHOD

1 Preheat the grill to 425°F (218°C) using direct heat with a cast iron grate installed and a cast iron skillet or an all-metal saucepan on the grate. Once hot, add butter to the skillet, stirring until melted, then stir in onion, ginger, and jalapeño. Sprinkle curry powder and ½ tsp salt over top and cook until onions begin to soften and brown, about 5 to 7 minutes, stirring occasionally.

2 Add tomatoes, cinnamon, lime leaves, and honey, pressing tomatoes with a wooden spoon to break them down. Cook uncovered until the sauce thickens and only a little liquid remains, about10 to 15 minutes, stirring occasionally.

3 Transfer the sauce to a blender (or use an immersion blender), and purée on high speed until smooth, about 1 minute. Wipe the skillet clean and return to the grill. Pour the sauce through a fine mesh strainer back into the skillet. Stir in cream and the remaining ½ tsp salt, adding more of each to taste.

4 Place paneer on the grate, close the lid, and cook until the cheese has visible grill marks, about 2 to 3 minutes per side. Cut into large cubes and add to the curry sauce. Gently stir in arugula and half the cilantro. Sprinkle the remaining cilantro over top, and serve immediately with warmed naan (if desired).

TIP

If you can't find paneer, you can substitute an equal amount of queso blanco. Look for a package labeled "for frying," which will hold its shape on the grill. Paneer is also easy to make at home.

BREADS & DESSERTS

PREP TIME
20 MINS

COOK TIME
35-45 MINS

SERVES
12

HEAT
INDIRECT
350ºF (177ºC)

COOKING SURFACE
STANDARD GRATE
METAL CAKE PAN

Dark, moist, and decadent, this cake has a rich chocolate flavor that's balanced by the slight bitterness of coffee. To save time, use a store-bought caramel sauce for the sweet-and-salty frosting.

CHOCOLATE CAKE
with salted caramel frosting

INGREDIENTS

2 cups all-purpose flour

2 cups sugar

²/₃ cup cocoa powder

2 tsp baking soda

1 tsp baking powder

1 tsp kosher salt

2 large eggs, at room temperature

1 cup buttermilk, at room temperature

1 cup strong black coffee, warm

½ cup vegetable oil

1 tbsp pure vanilla extract

flaky sea salt, for topping (optional)

for the caramel sauce

¾ cup sugar

4 tbsp water

4 tsp light corn syrup

¼ cup heavy cream

1 tsp pure vanilla extract

1½ tbsp unsalted butter

for the frosting

12 tbsp unsalted butter, at room temperature

2½ cups powdered sugar

1 tsp pure vanilla extract

1 tbsp heavy cream

kosher salt

METHOD

1 Preheat the grill to 350°F (177°C) using indirect heat with a standard grate installed. Grease a 9-in (23-cm) round metal cake pan with nonstick cooking spray and line with parchment paper. (Instead of a cake pan, you can also use a well-seasoned Dutch oven.)

2 In a large bowl or the bowl of a stand mixer, sift together flour, sugar, cocoa powder, baking soda, baking powder, and salt. In a separate medium bowl, whisk together eggs, buttermilk, coffee, vegetable oil, and vanilla extract.

3 Gradually add the liquid ingredients to the dry ingredients, stopping to scrape the sides and bottom of the bowl, until just combined. (The batter will be thin.) Pour the batter into the prepared cake pan or Dutch oven. Place on the grate, close the grill lid, and bake until a toothpick inserted in the center comes out almost clean, about 25 to 30 minutes. Let sit for 5 minutes, then turn out onto a wire rack to cool completely. (Use a butter knife to loosen the edges if needed.)

4 To make the caramel sauce, in a small saucepan, combine sugar, water, and corn syrup. Place on the stovetop over medium heat, and simmer until the mixture is deep amber in color, about 10 to 15 minutes. Slowly and carefully, add heavy cream, whisking constantly, then whisk in vanilla, butter, and a pinch of salt.

5 To make the frosting, in the bowl of a stand mixer fitted with the paddle attachment, beat butter on medium speed until light and fluffy, about 2 to 3 minutes. Add sugar, vanilla extract, heavy cream, and a pinch of salt. Beat on low speed until combined, about 1 minute. Increase the speed to medium-high and beat for 6 minutes. Add ½ cup caramel sauce and mix until combined.

6 Spread the frosting evenly over top and sides of the cooled cake, and drizzle with caramel sauce. Sprinkle with flaky sea salt (if desired) before serving.

PREP TIME
2 HRS

COOK TIME
5-6 MINS

SERVES
24

HEAT
**DIRECT
425°F (218°C)**

COOKING SURFACE
CAST IRON GRATE

This Indian-style flatbread is similar to a wood-fired pizza crust. Fresh from the grill, it's hot and chewy, with a crisp exterior and spots of charring. Serve it alongside your favorite curry or stew.

GRILLED NAAN

INGREDIENTS

1 cup warm water (105°F [41°C])

¼oz (7g) active dry yeast

¼ cup sugar

3 tbsp whole milk

1 large egg, beaten

2 tsp kosher salt

20¼oz (575g) bread flour, plus more for kneading

vegetable oil, for greasing

¼ cup butter, melted

METHOD

1 In a large bowl, combine water and yeast. Let sit until frothy, about 10 minutes. Stir in sugar, milk, egg, salt, and flour to make a soft dough. Knead on a lightly floured surface until smooth.

2 Lightly oil a large bowl, place the dough in the bowl, and cover with a damp cloth. Let sit to rise until the dough has doubled in volume, about 1 hour.

3 Punch the dough down and divide it into 4 balls (about the size of golf balls). Cover with a towel and allow to rise until the balls have doubled in size, about 30 minutes.

4 Preheat the grill to 425°F (218°C) using direct heat with a cast iron grate installed. Use a rolling pin one ball of dough into a thin circle. Lightly oil the grate, place the circle of dough on the grate, close the lid, and bake until puffy and lightly browned, about 2 to 3 minutes. Brush the uncooked side with butter, then flip the dough over and brush the cooked side with butter. Cook until puffy and lightly browned, about 3 minutes more. Repeat the cooking process with the remaining dough. (You can also bake all 4 balls at the same time.)

5 Remove the naan from the grill and sprinkle with seasoning of choice (if desired). Serve warm.

TIP
Before forming the dough into balls, add minced garlic, dried spices, or fresh herbs to the mix. Or take your naan in a sweet direction by adding cinnamon and sugar before or after cooking.

PREP TIME
3 DAYS

COOK TIME
20-25 MINS

MAKES
4 BAGUETTES

HEAT
INDIRECT
400°F (204°C)

COOKING SURFACE
STANDARD GRATE
PIZZA STONE

Homemade sourdough takes time, but the flavor is incomparable.
A three-day process develops a natural starter with no yeast
required. Once you've made the starter, you'll keep adding to it.

SOURDOUGH BAGUETTE

INGREDIENTS

cornmeal, for dusting

for Day 1 (starter)

8oz (225g) whole rye flour

8oz (235ml) warm water
 (105°F [41°C])

for Day 2

8oz (225g) bread flour

for Day 3

12oz (340g) bread flour

6oz (177ml) warm water
 (105°F [41°C])

8oz (225g) starter

for Day 4

3oz (85g) whole rye flour

31oz (915ml) warm water
 (105°F [41°C])

9½oz (270g) starter

42oz (1.2kg) bread flour

3oz (85g) whole wheat flour

1oz (25g) kosher salt

METHOD

1 On Day 1, in a large bowl, combine flour and water, cover tightly
with plastic wrap, and let sit overnight on the counter at warm room
temperature, about 70°F (21°C). (Cooler temperatures might inhibit
the growth of the starter.)

2 On Day 2, add flour to the starter and mix until a stiff, thick dough
forms. Cover tightly with plastic wrap and let sit overnight on the
counter at warm room temperature. The dough will rise overnight.

3 On Day 3, in a large bowl, combine flour, water, and 8 ounces (225g)
of the starter, and mix until a stiff, thick dough forms. Cover tightly
with plastic wrap and let sit overnight on the counter at warm room
temperature. The dough will rise overnight and should begin to
smell yeasty. (Freeze remaining starter for later use.)

4 On Day 4, preheat the grill to 400°F (204°C) using indirect heat with
a standard grate installed and a pizza stone on the grate. In a large
bowl, combine rye flour, water, 9½ ounces (270g) of the starter,
bread flour, wheat flour, and salt, and mix until a dough forms.
Cover tightly with plastic wrap and let sit for 20 minutes on the
counter. The dough will continue to smell yeasty. (Freeze remaining
starter for later use.)

5 Form the dough into 4 baguette shapes that are 10 to 12 inches
(25cm to 30.5cm) long and about 2½ inches (6.25cm) around.
Make 3 slits in the top of each loaf to allow steam to escape. Sprinkle
the pizza stone with cornmeal and place the loaves on the pizza
stone. Close the lid and bake until the bread reaches an internal
temperature of 190°F (88°C), about 20 to 25 minutes.

6 Remove the baguettes from the grill, place on a cutting board,
and let rest before slicing and serving as desired.

PREP TIME
8–24 HRS

COOK TIME
30–40 MINS

SERVES
8

HEAT
INDIRECT
425°F (218°C)

COOKING SURFACE
STANDARD GRATE
CAST IRON SKILLET

This rustic, chewy bread is studded with grilled corn kernels and bits of jalapeño. A garlic herb butter melts into the surface of the warm bread, infusing it with flavor and irresistible aroma.

CORN & JALAPEÑO FOCACCIA
with garlic herb butter

INGREDIENTS

2½ cups all-purpose or bread flour

1 tbsp kosher salt

½ tbsp instant dry yeast

1½ cups warm water (105°F [41°C])

3 tbsp extra virgin olive oil

3 jalapeño peppers, left whole

1 ear of corn, shucked

for the butter

1 tbsp olive oil

2 tbsp unsalted butter

4 garlic cloves, minced

2 tsp dried oregano

½ tsp red pepper flakes

kosher salt

METHOD

1 In a large bowl, combine flour, salt, yeast, and water. Cover tightly with plastic wrap, and set aside to rest for at least 8 hours and up to 24 hours. The dough will rise dramatically and fill the bowl.

2 Pour oil into a large cast iron skillet. Transfer the dough to the skillet, turning the dough to coat in oil. Press the dough around the skillet, flattening slightly and spreading to fill the entire bottom. Cover tightly with plastic wrap and let sit at room temperature for 2 hours.

3 After the first hour, preheat the grill to 425°F (218°C) using indirect heat with a standard grate installed. Place jalapeños and corn on the grate near the edges. Close the lid and grill until beginning to soften and char, about 10 to 12 minutes. Cut the kernels from the cob, and seed and dice jalapeños. Set aside.

4 After resting for 2 hours, the dough should mostly fill the skillet. Use your fingertips to firmly press the dough to the edges, popping any large bubbles that appear. Lift the dough at the edges and allow any air bubbles underneath to escape.

5 Evenly scatter corn and jalapeños over the dough, then push down until they're embedded in the dough. Place the skillet on the grate, close the grill lid, and bake until the top is golden brown and the bottom appears golden brown and crisp when lifted at the edge with a spatula, about 16 to 24 minutes.

6 To make the butter, on the stovetop in a small saucepan over medium-low heat, heat oil and butter until butter melts. Add garlic, oregano, and pepper flakes, and cook for 1 minute, stirring constantly. Transfer to a small bowl and season with salt to taste.

7 Transfer the focaccia to a cutting board and brush the butter over top. Allow to cool slightly, slice, and serve with any remaining butter.

PREP TIME
20 MINS

COOK TIME
20-25 MINS

MAKES
16 BISCUITS

HEAT
**INDIRECT
400°F (204°C)**

COOKING SURFACE
STANDARD GRATE

Almost nothing says "comfort food" like warm, mouth-watering biscuits. You can even freeze unbaked biscuits for up to 1 month to satisfy your craving for biscuits anytime.

BUTTERMILK BISCUITS

INGREDIENTS

4 cups all-purpose flour, plus more for rolling

½ cup nonfat powdered milk

4 tsp baking powder

1 tsp kosher salt

1 cup packed vegetable shortening

3 tbsp sour cream

3 tbsp buttermilk

3½oz (105ml) club soda

¼ cup butter, melted, for brushing

METHOD

1 Preheat the grill to 400°F (204°C) using indirect heat with a standard grate installed.

2 In a large bowl, sift together flour, powdered milk, baking powder, and salt. Using two forks or a pastry blender, cut in shortening until pea-sized pieces remain. In a separate large bowl, combine half the flour mixture with sour cream. Add buttermilk and club soda, and gently stir until just incorporated. Add remaining flour mixture, and stir until combined.

3 Place the dough on a well-floured work surface, gently roll out to ¾ in (2cm) thick, and generously flour the top. Using a 3-in (7.5-cm) biscuit cutter, cut out the biscuits and arrange on a parchment-lined baking pan.

4 Brush the biscuits liberally with melted butter, place the baking pan on the grate, close the lid, and bake until lightly golden brown, about 20 to 22 minutes. Remove the biscuits from the grill and serve warm.

PREP TIME
20 MINS

COOK TIME
30 MINS

SERVES
10

HEAT
INDIRECT
350ºF (177ºC)

COOKING SURFACE
STANDARD GRATE
CAST IRON SKILLET

Jewel-like berries crown the top of this upside-down cake, which is baked in a skillet on the grill. Use any combination of fresh seasonal berries, such as raspberries, currants, or blueberries.

BERRY UPSIDE-DOWN CAKE
with whipped cream & fresh mint

INGREDIENTS

10 tbsp unsalted butter,
   at room temperature, divided

1 cup packed light brown sugar,
   divided

11oz (315g) fresh seasonal berries

1 large egg

1 tsp pure vanilla extract

⅔ cup sour cream

1⅓ cups all-purpose flour

1 tbsp baking powder

¼ tsp baking soda

½ tsp kosher salt

¼ tsp ground cinnamon

fresh mint leaves, to garnish

whipped cream, to serve

METHOD

1 Preheat the grill to 350°F (177°C) using indirect heat with a standard grate installed and a cast iron skillet on the grate. Melt 2 tbsp butter in the skillet and swirl to coat. Remove the skillet from the grill. Sprinkle ⅓ cup brown sugar over butter, pour in berries, and shake the skillet until berries are evenly spread out. Set aside.

2 In the bowl of a stand mixer fitted with the paddle attachment, cream together remaining 8 tbsp butter and ⅔ cup brown sugar until fluffy. Add egg, vanilla, and sour cream, and beat to combine.

3 In a medium bowl, sift together flour, baking powder, baking soda, salt, and cinnamon. Gradually add the dry ingredients to the butter and egg mixture until just incorporated. (The batter will be thick.) Using a rubber spatula, scoop the batter into the skillet, smoothing it over berries.

4 Place the skillet on the grate, close the lid, and bake until golden brown and a cake tester inserted into the middle of the cake comes out clean, about 30 minutes. Remove the skillet from the grill and place on a wire rack to cool for 15 minutes.

5 To serve, flip the cake upside down on a large serving platter and release from the skillet, leaving the berries on top. Garnish with fresh mint leaves, and serve with a dollop of whipped cream.

PREP TIME
20 MINS

COOK TIME
50-55 MINS

SERVES
8

HEAT
**INDIRECT
350°F (177°C)**

COOKING SURFACE
**STANDARD GRATE
METAL PIE PAN**

This simple and adaptable open-faced pie lends itself to many seasonal fruit varieties. In the early fall, sweet Seckel pears and tart red plums make a beautiful, rosy-hued filling.

GRILLED FRUIT PIE

INGREDIENTS

for the crust

1 cup all-purpose flour, plus extra for rolling dough

½ tsp kosher salt

½ cup butter, chilled and cut into small cubes

¼ cup ice water

2lb (1kg) dried beans, for blind baking

powdered sugar, for dusting

whipped cream or ice cream, to serve (optional)

for the filling

1¼lb (565g) seasonal fruit, such as pears and plums, halved and pitted

½ cup sugar

4 tbsp cornstarch

2 tbsp lemon juice

METHOD

1 Preheat the grill to 350°F (177°C) using indirect heat with a standard grate installed. Place fruit on the grate skin side up, keeping them toward the edges of the grate. Close the lid and grill until beginning to soften, about 3 to 5 minutes. Transfer to a cutting board and slice. Set aside.

2 To make the crust, in a food processor, combine flour and salt, pulsing 3 to 4 times. Add butter, and pulse until the texture is mealy, about 5 to 6 times. With the food processor running, slowly add the ice water in 1 tbsp increments until the dough comes together.

3 Turn out the dough onto a floured work surface and sprinkle with flour. Using a rolling pin, roll dough out to a 10- to 11-in (25- to 28-cm) circle. Carefully transfer the dough to a 9-in (23-cm) metal pie pan, pressing the dough to the edges. Trim any overhang and crimp the edges. Prick the dough with a fork to prevent bubbles during baking. Place the pan in the fridge to chill for 15 minutes.

4 Spread a large piece of parchment paper over the dough and fill the pan with dry beans, pressing them into the edges of the dough. Place the pan on the grate, close the lid, and bake for 10 minutes. Remove the parchment and beans from the pan, and continue baking the crust until golden brown in color, about 10 to 15 minutes more. Remove the pan from the grill and let the crust cool completely before filling.

5 To make the filling, in a large bowl, combine sugar, cornstarch, and juice. Add the grilled fruit and toss lightly to coat. Pour the fruit mixture into the baked crust. Place on the grate, close the lid, and bake until the filling is thickened and bubbling at the edges, about 30 minutes.

6 Remove the pie from the grill and place on a wire rack to cool. Just before serving, sprinkle with powdered sugar. Serve with whipped cream or ice cream (if desired).

PREP TIME
30 MIN

COOK TIME
40–45 MIN

SERVES
16

HEAT
INDIRECT
350°F (177°C)

COOKING SURFACE
STANDARD GRATE

This almond-flavored cake has the light fluffiness of angel food cake but with a richer taste. The almond buttercream frosting is made with flour for a light, smooth, and silky texture.

ALMOND CREAM CAKE

INGREDIENTS

2 cups butter, softened

3 cups sugar

6 cups cake flour

1 tsp kosher salt

4 tsp baking powder

2 cups whole milk

2 tsp almond extract

10 large eggs, whites only

sliced almonds, to decorate

for the frosting

1¼ cups all-purpose flour

2 cups whole milk

½ tsp almond extract

1 tbsp vanilla bean paste

2 cups butter, softened

2 cups sugar

METHOD

1 In the bowl of a stand mixer fitted with the paddle attachment, cream butter until white in appearance. Add sugar and beat until fluffy. In a large bowl, sift together flour, salt, and baking powder. Add the flour mixture to the butter mixture in three stages, alternating with the milk and almond extract and mixing after each addition until just combined.

2 In a large bowl, beat egg whites until they form stiff peaks. Using a spatula, gently fold egg whites into the cake batter, taking care not to overmix.

3 Preheat the grill to 350°F (177°C) using indirect heat with a standard grate installed. Line an 11 x 18-in (28 x 46cm) grill-safe baking pan with parchment paper and lightly grease with cooking spray. Pour the batter into the pan, place on the grate, close the lid, and bake until the top springs back when touched, about 27 to 30 minutes.

4 Remove the cake from the grill and place on a wire rack to cool for 10 minutes. Use a knife to loosen the edges, and transfer the cake to a wire rack to cool completely.

5 To make the frosting, on the stovetop in a saucepan over medium-low heat, whisk together flour and milk until mixture thickens to the consistency of mashed potatoes, about 12 to 15 minutes. Stir constantly, and lower the heat if needed. Remove the saucepan from the heat and place in a bowl of ice for 5 to 10 minutes to hasten the cooling process and bring the mixture to room temperature. Once cool, stir in almond extract.

6 In the bowl of a stand mixer, cream together vanilla paste, butter, and sugar until the mixture is light and fluffy and sugar is completely dissolved. Add the flour mixture, and beat until it has the appearance of whipped cream, scraping the sides of the bowl as needed.

7 Spread the frosting evenly over the cooled cake and sprinkle sliced almonds over top to decorate before serving.

PREP TIME
20 MINS

COOK TIME
1½ HRS

SERVES
12

HEAT
**INDIRECT
350°F (177°C)**

COOKING SURFACE
STANDARD GRATE

This dessert—with hints of brown butter and savory fruit—can deliciously complete a meal. This recipe is versatile enough to use almost any fruit, including berries, stone fruits, apples, or pears.

SEASONAL FRUIT COBBLER

INGREDIENTS

2lb (1kg) seasonal fruit, washed, pitted (if needed), and sliced or halved if needed

½ tsp ground cinnamon

2 tsp cornstarch (for juicy fruits; omit for pears or apples)

4 tbsp butter, plus more for greasing

½ cup sugar, plus more for sprinkling

¾ cup self-rising flour

¾ cup whole milk

whipped cream, to serve

METHOD

1 Preheat the grill to 350°F (177°C) using indirect heat with a standard grate installed. Place the fruit on the grate (or in a cast iron skillet if the fruit might fall through the grate), close the lid, and grill until beginning to soften and char, about 7 to 10 minutes. Remove fruit from the grill and place in a large bowl. Sprinkle cinnamon and cornstarch (if using) over fruit, and add a little sugar (if desired). Gently toss to coat and set aside.

2 Grease a 9-in (23-cm) grill-safe baking pan with butter. On the stovetop in a small saucepan, heat 4 tbsp butter over medium-low heat until beginning to brown, about 10 to 15 minutes.

3 In a medium bowl, whisk together butter, sugar, flour, and milk. Transfer fruit to the prepared baking pan and spread the batter evenly over top. Place the pan on the grate, close the lid, and bake until golden brown and bubbly, about 1 hour. In the last 10 minutes of cooking, sprinkle a light amount of sugar over top. Remove the cobbler from the grill, and serve warm with whipped cream on top.

TIP For the best flavor, use fresh fruit at the peak of ripeness. Try a mix of stone fruits and berries or use several different apple varieties. Adjust the spices as needed to suit the fruit you select.

PREP TIME **2-4 HRS**	COOK TIME **4-6 MINS**	SERVES **2**	HEAT **DIRECT** **600°F (315°C)**	COOKING SURFACE **PIZZA STONE**

The high heat of the kamado grill makes it possible to achieve the crisp-yet-chewy crust of a Neapolitan-style pizza, topped here with the classic combination of tomato, basil, and mozzarella.

PIZZA MARGHERITA

INGREDIENTS

cornmeal, for dusting

¼ cup marinara sauce

2oz (55g) fresh mozzarella, sliced

3 garlic cloves, thinly sliced

12–16 fresh basil leaves

kosher salt and freshly ground
black pepper

grated Parmesan, to serve

for the dough

12oz (340g) Italian 00 flour,
plus more for dusting

4 tsp kosher salt

2 tsp instant dry yeast

6½oz (190ml) warm water
(105°F [41°C])

METHOD

1 To make the dough, in a large bowl, whisk together flour, salt, and yeast until well combined. Add water, and use your hands to mix until no dry flour remains. Cover tightly with plastic wrap and allow to rise at room temperature for 2 to 4 hours. Turn the dough out onto a lightly floured surface and allow to sit at room temperature for 2 hours before baking.

2 Preheat the grill to 600°F (316°C) using indirect heat with a pizza stone resting directly on the heat deflector. (The pizza stone should be level with the grill rim.)

3 On a lightly floured work surface, roll out the dough to ¼ in (.5cm) thick and a 10-in (25cm) diameter. Lightly dust a pizza paddle or unrimmed baking sheet with cornmeal, and place the dough on top. Evenly spread the sauce over the dough, working from the center to the edges. Top with the sliced mozzarella and garlic.

4 Carefully slide the pizza from the paddle to the hot pizza stone. Close the lid and bake until the crust is golden brown and the cheese is melted and beginning to bubble, about 4 to 6 minutes.

5 Use the pizza paddle to remove the pizza from the grill. Scatter the basil leaves over top and sprinkle with salt, pepper, and Parmesan.

 TIP It's worth the effort to seek out Italian 00 flour, which is more finely ground than all-purpose flour, yielding an exceptional crust.

INDEX

DEDICATION
I dedicate this book to my mom and dad, to Lala and Poppy, to Jim and Laurel, and to Ryan Z. Your love, wisdom, and support made this possible. Thank you.

ABOUT THE AUTHOR
Hailing from the gorgeous Pacific Northwest, JJ Boston grew up appreciating the beauty of his environment and the simplicity of fresh, local food. He stayed true to his roots through more than 17 years working in fine restaurants across the country. Founded in 2005, Chef JJ's business has grown from a personal chef platform into what's now a hugely popular dining experience in Indianapolis.

Chef JJ has made the kamado grill the centerpiece of his two successful Indianapolis restaurants: Chef JJ's Back Yard and Chef JJ's Downtown. Both locations have quickly become popular destinations for private events, corporate team building, and grilling classes—all featuring meals prepared on the Big Green Egg, the most recognizable kamado-style grill on the market. The two locations now host thousands of clients each month for interactive grilling experiences with the Big Green Egg.

Chef JJ lives in Indianapolis with his wife and two children. They operate two restaurant locations and two urban farms, where they produce fruits, vegetables, and herbs.

AUTHOR'S ACKNOWLEDGMENTS
Thanks to my wife, Sarah; our sons, Tanner and Jack; and my right-hand man, Boyd. Thanks also to the recipe testers, Lee and Max; the entire DK publishing staff; and the amazing team at Chef JJ's who worked on this project: Erica, Omar, Ricardo, Chef Shua, Chef Anthony, meat monger Kevin, and cheese monger Katie. And thanks to all the past and present chefs I've worked with who have inspired me.

PUBLISHER'S ACKNOWLEDGMENTS
DK Publishing and Alpha Books would like to thank the following:
Food stylist: Lovoni Walker
Lighting director: JD Schuyler
Food testers: Lee Rosser and Max Skillman
Proofreader: Lisa Starnes
Indexer: Celia McCoy

Penguin
Random
House

Publisher Mike Sanders
Editors Ann Barton and Christopher Stolle
Book Designer Lindsay Dobbs
Art Director William Thomas
Photographer Kelley Schuyler

First American Edition, 2018
Published in the United States by DK Publishing
6081 E. 82nd Street, Indianapolis, Indiana 46250

Copyright © 2018 Dorling Kindersley Limited
DK, a Division of Penguin Random House LLC
18 19 20 21 22   10 9 8 7 6 5 4 3 2 1
001–309808–May/2018

Published in the United States by Dorling Kindersley Limited

Note: This publication contains the opinions and ideas of its author(s).
It is intended to provide helpful and informative material on the subject
matter covered. It is sold with the understanding that the author(s) and
publisher are not engaged in rendering professional services in the
book. If the reader requires personal assistance or advice, a competent
professional should be consulted. The author(s) and publisher
specifically disclaim any responsibility for any liability, loss, or risk,
personal or otherwise, which is incurred as a consequence, directly or
indirectly, of the use and application of any of the contents of this book.

Trademarks: All terms mentioned in this book that are known to be
or are suspected of being trademarks or service marks have been
appropriately capitalized. Alpha Books, DK, and Penguin Random
House LLC cannot attest to the accuracy of this information. Use of
a term in this book should not be regarded as affecting the validity
of any trademark or service mark.

A catalog record for this book
is available from the Library of Congress.
ISBN 978-1-4654-7353-0
Library of Congress Catalog Number: 2017956788

DK books are available at special discounts when purchased
in bulk for sales promotions, premiums, fund-raising, or educational
use. For details, contact: DK Publishing Special Markets, 345 Hudson
Street, New York, New York 10014
SpecialSales@dk.com

Printed and bound in China

All images © Dorling Kindersley Limited
For further information see: www.dkimages.com

A WORLD OF IDEAS:
SEE ALL THERE IS TO KNOW

www.dk.com